THE CIVIL WAR

EXPERIENCE

1861-1865

JAY WERTZ

SEVENOAKS

MAP KEY

CONTENTS

THIS MAP KEY contains the symbols used, as indicated, in 15 maps in this book that demonstrate the placement and movement of units as well as actions in many of the significant battles and campaigns of the Civil War.

Designation	Confederate Army	Federal Army
army headquarters		
Grand Division	BEAUREGARD	HOOKER
army	LEE	GRANT
corps (with number)	JACKSON	SHERMAN
cavalry corps	FORREST	SHERIDAN
division	McLAWS	DOUBLEDAY
advance	→	→
retreat	---→	---→
brigade or less		
artillery		
fort		
siege line or fortification		

Area Maps (Trans-Mississippi, Mississippi River)	
Union Victory	
Confederate Victory	
Inconclusive	

Campaign Maps (Vicksburg, Atlanta)	
Engagements	

THE WAR THAT MADE AMERICA

ABOUT THE TIME the first shots of the Civil War were fired at Fort Sumter in 1861, participants, journalists, and observers began to write about their personal experiences and what they saw happening around them. Thus, the process had begun of making the Civil War the most written-about period in American history. Since that time scholars, writers, and enthusiasts have explored in detail every aspect of the period. The speculation on how just a few differences could have altered the outcome of the war is endless.

Why has this period produced such a never-ending fascination? For many Americans the answer is quite simple—it's a very personal war. Interest in the Civil War often begins with proximity to battlefields or a family connection, perhaps with an artifact, diary, or letters left behind and handed down through the generations. The connection can be quite partisan too, because Americans fighting Americans naturally produced close enemies—friend against friend, neighbor against neighbor, brother against brother.

For the world at large, the continuing interest in the Civil War is also well explained. Although the nation was born in the late 1700s, and its emergence was preserved by the Revolutionary War, even the drafting of the United States Constitution could not truly heal the strong sectional differences. That process would ultimately have to be achieved on the battlefields of the Civil War, after decades of political compromise and individual actions had failed. As Dr. James McPherson, Pulitzer Prize-winning scholar of the period, has observed, without the Civil War and the resulting victory for the Union, the United States would have gone the way of Latin America—becoming a group of smaller nations with much longer gestation periods and varying results in the quest for democracy. Clearly, the history of the entire world would have changed if that scenario had played out.

This multi-faceted work brings a new perspective to Civil War studies, both for those who have an in-depth

knowledge of the war and those who are just beginning to read about the period. The inclusion of facsimile documents, ranging from great national treasures to personal items, and audio transcriptions of the words of participants and observers, helps one to understand the depth of commitment made by the Union and Confederate soldiers and those civilians touched by the others with roles in the war. The drama and ironies of this national struggle are evident as each event is explored. The Civil War is often said to be the first modern war—the first time invention and technology had a major impact on strategy and tactics, and, at times, affected the outcome of contests. But it was, like all wars, primarily a saga of the people involved, a war of heroics and blunders, of struggle and pain. When a woman in the path of his army soldiers asked him why soldiers took food with no permission or compensation, William T. Sherman replied, with reference to his oft-used theme, "Madam, my soldiers must subsist themselves even if the whole country must be ruined to maintain them. War is cruelty. There is no use trying to reform it; the crueler it is, the sooner it will be over."

War is indeed a cruel enterprise. The study of or interest in it is not. An understanding of the Civil War and the roles played in it by those who came before us is vital if we are to prevent the recurrence of the inhuman attitudes that were a major cause of the conflict. The dedication of those soldiers and leaders made America what it is. Perhaps we owe it to them to know something about their lives, deeds, and what they stood for, because if they had not answered the call of duty, we might be living in a more terrible place.

JAY WERTZ

THE UNION DISSOLVED

APRIL 12, 1861 was the day the United States ceased to be one nation united, and embarked on a four-year civil war. The previous December, South Carolina had seceded from the Union, and in the next few months, six other Southern states joined together to form a confederacy in which state sovereignty reigned.

The tension between North and South that led to the formation of the Confederate States of America went back more than half a century. Since the early part of the 19th century, the agrarian states of the South had come under increasing fire for their use of slave labor. As the young country expanded westward, abolitionists in the North tried to limit the spread of slavery. Starting with the Missouri Compromise of 1820, congressional action created interim settlements that quickly broke down.

The first shot in the conflict was symbolically fired in November of 1860 with the election of Abraham Lincoln as President. Lincoln, representing the new antislavery Republican Party, had in fact no intention of abolishing slavery in the South when he took office, but South Carolina interpreted his election as a sign of the increasing shift of Federal political power away from the proslavery South. The citizens of Charleston began harassment of the U.S. Army garrison stationed at Fort Moultrie in Charleston Harbor, which, together with Castle Pinckney, about a mile off the waterfront, and Fort Sumter, at the mouth of the harbor, represented the Federal military presence in the city.

The newly arrived commander of the three forts was Major Robert Anderson. He made urgent requests to Washington for supplies and reinforcements, but little help came from President James Buchanan, a weak, lame-duck figure who wished to delay the crisis until after he left office, or Secretary of War John Floyd, a Southerner sympathetic to secession.

April 12–14, 1861

ABRAHAM LINCOLN

In many ways, Abraham Lincoln was as instrumental in saving the Union as the battlefield victories of the North. He may have peered too far as Commander-in-Chief into the day-to-day activities of the military, but his instincts in that direction were valid. He was able to evaluate talent and apply just enough pressure on those generals who had what it took, while replacing those who did not. In handling the delicate political situation during the war, Lincoln had no equal.

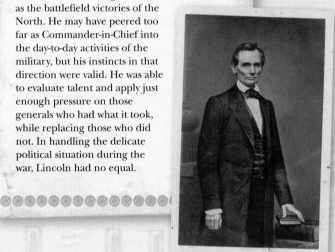

Abraham Lincoln

LEFT Federal guns fire from inside Fort Sumter in this period lithograph. The fort was designed to defend against ships entering Charleston Harbor, so most of the cannons inside the fort had limited effect against the Rebel shore batteries.

Lacking a definitive order to defend Fort Moultrie, Anderson moved its garrison to Fort Sumter on the evening of 26 December 1860.

Even though Anderson viewed the move to Fort Sumter as delaying confrontation, Southerners viewed the appearance of the Stars and Stripes over the fort as an act of aggression. By the time Lincoln took office on March 4, 1861, the construction of the Charleston batteries under the command of Brigadier General Pierre Gustave Toutant Beauregard was nearly complete. "We are not enemies, but friends. We must not be enemies," Lincoln implored in his inaugural address. But it was too late for conciliation. Anderson was running out of supplies, and to relieve him, a mission would have to be sent to Fort Sumter.

The head of the Confederate government, former Mississippi senator Jefferson Davis, convened his cabinet in Montgomery, Alabama, and together they concluded that Fort Sumter must not be resupplied. Any other position would have risked a loss of faith in the new government.

On April 11, Beauregard received word from Montgomery to deliver a surrender ultimatum to Anderson. Former South Carolina senator James Chesnut, now a colonel on Beauregard's staff, was charged with delivering the message by rowing out to the fort. Anderson declined to surrender, but he hinted to Chesnut that without supplies the Federal garrison might soon be forced to give up the fort. This "rowboat" diplomacy dragged on into the early hours of the 12th. Finally, at 3.30 a.m., Chesnut informed Anderson that bombardment of the fort would commence in one hour. A cannon was then readied to give the signal for the firing to commence. The lanyard was offered to outspoken secessionist Roger Pryor, who declined to pull it. So Lieutenant Henry Farley did, at 4.30 a.m. on April 12, 1861.

For several hours the confederate battering around the harbor received no answering fire from Fort Sumter. When the Federals finally opened fire at about 7.00 a.m., their solid shot, meant for sinking an invading armada, did little damage to the well-protected Confederate guns. A squadron of ships sent to resupply the fort arrived off the Charleston bar shortly before the start of the bombardment, but planning errors, indecision, and poor sea conditions prevented any of the supplies from reaching Sumter. The fort, meanwhile, was holding up reasonably well, having withstood more than 3,000 shots. However, fires in the fort's wooden buildings created difficult and dangerous conditions for the garrison. An honorable surrender was worked out between Anderson and Beauregard's representatives before the 33-hour bombardment ended.

The Federal garrison left Charleston on the resupply ships and a telegraph dispatch informed Lincoln and the nation of Fort Sumter's surrender and the end of peace in an undivided union.

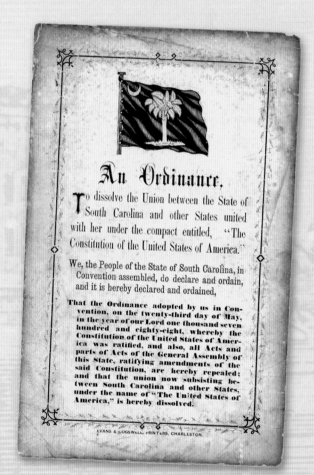

JEFFERSON DAVIS

Davis was a reluctant President of the Confederacy, but having accepted the job, he performed it with gusto. A West Point graduate and former Secretary of War, he at times micromanaged the military, clashing frequently with his top generals. He often sought the advice of General Robert E. Lee, who advised him on strategy and resource management. Like Lincoln, Davis had to contend with a legislature that was frequently divided and "political generals," whose agendas rarely had the good of the state as their first priority.

ABOVE As this commemorative copy of South Carolina's Ordinance of Secession illustrates, leaders there believed that the United States Constitution was a contract that individual states could break.

BACKGROUND Fort Sumter in a prewar lithograph. The fort was a Third System coastal fortification begun in 1829 on a man-made island of New England granite.

SLAVERY AND THE ABOLITIONISTS

THE PRINCIPAL CAUSE of the American Civil War was the division between the Federal government and people of the North and the Southern states and their citizens over the issue of slavery. As the United States expanded westward, these differences also grew. Influencing the Federal government at this time were the abolitionists, a diverse group who found the institution of slavery morally objectionable. They were in direct philosophical opposition to the slave-holders and politicians of the South.

The plantation system of the South depended on African slaves brought to America during the nation's infancy, and later their American-born descendants. The staple crops of cotton, tobacco, rice, and sugar were labor- and mineral-intensive. To meet the demand for labor, and despite the fact that the United States banned the slave trade after 1807, the illegal importation of slaves continued, and a domestic market in slaves developed.

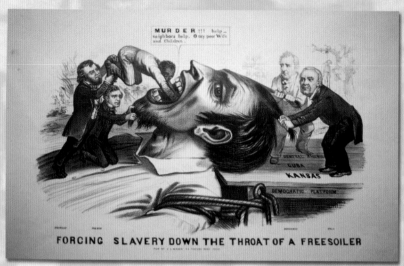

FORCING SLAVERY DOWN THE THROAT OF A FREESOILER

ABOVE An 1856 Republican cartoon that satirized Democratic support of popular sovereignty in Kansas. Even though intimidation and election irregularity resulted in a vote allowing slavery, only two slaves were in the state by 1860. The climate and terrain of Kansas were poorly suited to Southern staple crops.

LEFT Slaves separating cotton on the Smith plantation in Virginia. The cotton gin and other advancements in processing the fiber did not reduce the producers' use of slave labor.

BACKGROUND Plantation slaves lived in small cabins, like those in this photograph. Children too young to work entertained themselves while adults labored.

Lowly, an 1852 novel by Harriet Beecher Stowe. It was a bestseller, and the most talked-about book of its time.

A second method was through political action. Beginning in 1819, with Congressman James Tallmadge's resolution to prohibit slavery in Missouri as a condition for that territory's becoming a state, the slavery question fostered a number of measures and compromises. The Republican Party was born from amongst those opposed to slavery's expansion and those who called for the abolition of slavery where it existed. Slavery was the main political issue that divided Congress, weakened the Democratic Party, challenged the Supreme Court, and which was instrumental in the election of the first Republican President.

Many slave owners deluded themselves into thinking that they were benevolent providers. James Hammond, a South Carolina politician and slave-owner, defined slaves as the necessary "mudsill of society," and suggested that the South's slaves were better treated than the North's unskilled factory workers. Yet even those slaves who became skilled artisans, or worked in domestic capacities, endured the despair and degradation that came from fear, punishment, family separation, and often-inhumane treatment.

In this environment the abolitionists grew in number and power. The abolitionist movement impacted events leading to the Civil War in four ways. The first and most widespread was public awareness. Through speeches, rallies, and publications, individuals and groups proclaimed the evils of slavery. Wendell Phillips, John Greenleaf Whittier, and William Lloyd Garrison, among many others, sought to influence public and political action through speeches and writings, as did the ex-slaves Frederick Douglass and Sojourner Truth. Arguably the most influential publication was, *Uncle Tom's Cabin: or, Life among the*

JOHN BROWN

Brown was a deeply religious drifter who saw slavery as a sin against God. He spoke openly of violence and began to carry out his punishing vendettas against proslavery Kansas settlers in 1856. Committed to organizing a slave uprising, he surreptitiously received funding from the "Secret Six," a group of wealthy patrons. He escaped legal incarceration over the "Pottawatomie Massacre" and moved east to plan his next move. Universally condemned for his Harpers Ferry raid, Brown's death brought the forces opposing slavery closer together.

CHARLES SUMNER

A leading "Radical Republican," the Harvard-educated Boston lawyer was first elected to the U.S. Senate on a coalition ticket in 1851, but was reelected as a Republican in 1857. He was an early opponent of compromise measures on slavery and his May 1856 speech "The Crime Against Kansas" was openly critical of Senator Stephen A. Douglas and others. Sumner and other Republicans took a hard line against Southern reincorporation into the Union, though he softened this stance somewhat after a visit to the devastated South.

"I appear this evening as a thief and a robber. I stole this head, these limbs, this body from my master, and ran off with them."

FREDERICK DOUGLASS IN AN ANTEBELLUM SPEECH TO ABOLITIONISTS

The third way in which the abolitionists impacted slavery was in the aiding of runaway slaves. In the three decades before the Civil War, the "underground railroad" was a way for escaped slaves to disappear into Northern society. It was actually a series of safe houses and means of transportation operated by volunteers sympathetic to the plight of the slaves. The process was made more dangerous when the Compromise of 1850 resulted in the enactment of the Fugitive Slave Law, which gave Federal commissioners the power to arrest runaway slaves. Professional slave hunters used the law to scour Northern cities for runaways, rounding up many free African-Americans in the process. In response, abolitionists extended the "underground railroad" all the way to Canada.

The final method explored the dark side of abolition: violence. Vigilante committees sprang up and clashed with those enforcing the Fugitive Slave Law. The Kansas-Nebraska bill of 1854, introduced by Senator Stephen A. Douglas of Illinois, called for these territories to be admitted as free or slave states as their constitutions prescribed. When the bill became law, pro- and antislavery factions rushed to populate Kansas and exert political power. Blood was spilled as a result of the lawlessness which ensued. The most famous of these incidents involved John Brown, who murdered five proslavery men in cold blood. Then, in 1859, Brown put his planned slave uprising in motion by taking the United States arsenal at Harpers Ferry, Virginia. No slave uprising occurred, but Brown was captured, tried, convicted, and hanged.

THE BATTLE OF FIRST MANASSAS

July 21, 1861

AFTER PRESIDENT LINCOLN'S proclamation on April 15, 1861 declaring an insurrection against the laws of the United States and his call for "ninety-day volunteers to put down the rebellion," both sides spent months building their military forces. In widely scattered places such as Big Bethel, Virginia, and Boonville, Missouri, isolated engagements occurred but in July, under public and political pressure from those impatient with General-in-Chief Winfield Scott's grand strategy for defeating the South, Federal leaders decided to strike a decisive blow at Richmond, Virginia, the Confederacy's capital.

Scott was too old for battlefield command and so Brigadier General Irvin McDowell, a West Pointer with little command experience, was appointed field commander. With many of the enlistments of the 90-day volunteers due to expire, McDowell's force of 35,000—which also included U.S. Regular Army infantry, artillery, and cavalry, and Marine Corps battalions—left Washington on July 16.

An opposing Confederate force of 22,000 under Brigadier General P.G.T. Beauregard, the "Hero of Sumter," was situated 25 miles southwest of Washington, guarding the important railroad junction at Manassas. The other two principal forces in the area were 18,000 Federals under Major General Robert Patterson at Harpers Ferry, and about 12,000 Rebels under General Joseph E. Johnston guarding the Shenandoah Valley at Winchester.

McDowell's novice force moved slowly, stopping along the way to replenish their supplies. Beauregard, hearing of the Federal advance, asked Richmond for reinforcements to strengthen his seven-mile defense line south of Bull Run. At the same time Johnston dispatched troops from Winchester to board trains for Manassas, while a small cavalry force under Colonel J.E.B. Stuart screened the operation from Patterson's

THE SPRINGFIELD MUSKET

The Springfield Musket was the most widely available weapon for Civil War soldiers. It was a cap and ball weapon that fired a 55mm projectile. The 1861 design was manufactured at the Federal armory in Springfield, Massachusetts, and by independent contractors in the North. During the course of the war, 1.2 million of the rifle-muskets were made. In the South, a variation of the Springfield was made at Richmond using machinery seized from the other rifle-making U.S. armory at Harpers Ferry.

force. Patterson was fooled, and his failure to hold Johnston in place would affect the outcome at First Manassas.

By the 18th, the head of McDowell's force arrived at Centreville, just northeast of Bull Run. Against orders, the division's commander, Brigadier General Daniel Tyler, probed the Confederate positions at Blackburn's Ford and a lively skirmish ensued. McDowell, fearing the action would cause the Confederates to reinforce their right flank, changed his strategy and sent engineers to search for crossing points to the north.

On July 20, Johnston arrived at Manassas with the lead elements of his force. By virtue of rank, Johnston took command

RIGHT The Federal move to Sudley Ford might have succeeded—the Confederates were planning an advance on Blackburn's Ford—had Signal Officer Capt. E. Porter Alexander not seen the glint of Union bayonets and warned his superiors.

BELOW The capture of Capt. James D. Ricketts's battery by the 33rd Virginia infantry. These guns and another Federal battery were captured and recaptured throughout the day.

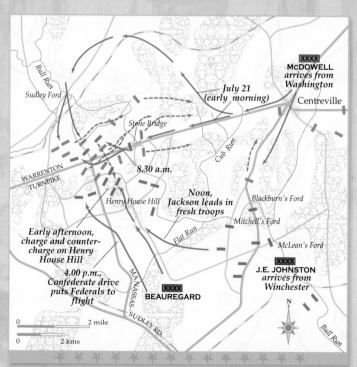

RAILROADS IN THE CIVIL WAR

The military use of railroads is among the reasons the Civil War is considered the first modern war. Dramatic troop movements, such as those at First Manassas and Chickamauga, illustrated the possibilities of rapid deployment, but supplies were the principal cargo. Railroads were vulnerable to raids and sabotage. The South had additional problems: varying track gauge and scarcity of replacement parts. Both sides had to deal with independent railroad companies. As a result, the North established a military rail system in 1862.

"Our army was more disorganized by victory than that of the United States by defeat."

GENERAL JOSEPH E. JOHNSTON EXPLAINING TO PRESIDENT DAVIS WHY THEY DID NOT PURSUE THE ENEMY AFTER THE BATTLE

RIGHT Ruins of the Stone Bridge over Bull Run in 1862, looking southwest toward the initial position of Evans's Brigade.

BELOW LEFT Gen. Joseph E. Johnston, CSA, acted as overall commander and directed reinforcements to key positions in the battle.

BELOW AND BACKGROUND Col. Ambrose E. Burnside's brigade overtakes Confederates on Matthews Hill in the battle's opening phase.

of the Confederates, though he allowed Beauregard to submit a battle plan, which called for an attack on the enemy left.

In the pre-dawn hours of Sunday, July 21, two of McDowell's divisions inched toward Sudley and Poplar Fords, but their progress was hampered by poor logistics and thick underbrush. McDowell's other units fanned out along the creek. At 6.00 a.m., Tyler initiated the battle with artillery fire directed at Rebel units across the Stone Bridge. As Colonel Nathan Evans's force returned fire, Federal units were sighted to the north. These two Federal divisions, led by Colonel Ambrose E. Burnside's Rhode Island volunteers, moved south to

advance, but committed his artillery too far forward on Henry Hill and it was captured. The varied uniforms of the new armies, which included elements on both sides dressed in enemy colors, added to the confusion. By 3.00 p.m., with the last Northern troops committed to the fight on Henry Hill, the tide turned against them. Johnston continued to send fresh troops to the front, and the Federals began to retreat to the east over the Stone Bridge. The withdrawal turned into a rout that became a free-for-all when a wagon overturned, blocking Cub Run Bridge.

Although the Federal retreat extended all the way to Washington, the Confederates, being in a state of some disorganization, did not pursue. Though casualties were small compared to later battles— approximately 3,400 killed, wounded, and missing on both sides—the defeat caused an uproar in the North. McDowell and Beauregard both made the mistake of committing forces piecemeal. However, Beauregard was reinforced by Johnston, while McDowell failed effectively to marshal his ill-prepared force and was unsupported by Patterson's failure to hold Johnston. McDowell was relieved of his command. This defeat and another, three months later at Ball's Bluff, Virginia, resulted in harsh Congressional criticism of the military, and paved the way for new leadership under George B. McClellan.

Matthews Hill. They succeeded in driving Evans's men back, but then paused. Meanwhile, Brigadier Thomas J. Jackson joined others in hastening to occupy Henry Hill to the south.

As Confederate units under Evans and others fell back from Matthews Hill, one of their commanders, Brigadier General Barnard Bee, remarked how Jackson and his men stood "like a stone wall," on Henry Hill, making the location a rallying point for the retreating Rebels.

Beauregard and Johnston abandoned the offensive on the Confederate right and rode to Henry Hill. McDowell started to

RIGHT Brig. Gen. Irvin McDowell, USA, lost twice at the battlefield along Bull Run. The second defeat was as a corps commander in the Battle of Second Manassas.

CIVIL WAR FORCES AND STRATEGIES

slavery. For the South the end of the war was imagined as giving birth to a new nation, the Confederate States of America. However, it soon became apparent to both sides that the Civil War would have to be resolved through the defeat of armies, the occupation of territory, and, at the end, a single victor.

This did not mean the two sides did not seek alternatives to total war and total victory. At the beginning of the war, General-in-Chief Winfield Scott proposed blockading the ports of the South and taking control of the Mississippi River to divide the Confederacy in two. He reasoned that the South would then realize just how much it depended on the North for survival. That did not happen, but elements of Scott's plan formed the foundation for subsequent Northern war strategy.

For its part, the South hoped to force an armistice that would allow it to leave the Union in peace. To do this the Confederates

BELOW The press derided Winfield Scott's early-war plan to strangle the Confederacy with a naval blockade and take control of the Mississippi. However, elements of Scott's plan became part of Federal strategy.

THE CIVIL WAR was different from earlier 19th-century wars. The two enemies spoke the same language, and shared a similar—if not identical—heritage. In the beginning, both sides believed that swift victory would lead to a cessation of hostilities and a political solution. For the North that meant a return of Southern states to the Union with new limitations on the expansion of

ABOVE Robert E. Lee as a U.S. Army officer. He was described as "the best soldier I ever saw in the field," by General Winfield Scott, to whom he submitted his resignation.

BELOW Soldiers in dress militia uniforms pose before going to war.

FEDERAL UNIFORMS

The uniform standards for Federal army, navy, and marine officers and soldiers were detailed in official regulations as to color, style, and trim, but these rules were not always rigorously enforced. By 1863, the varied dress of some volunteer regiments gave way to the Regular Army uniform: dark blue wool frock or sack coat worn over sky-blue trousers, kepi or forage hat, ankle-high boots, and leather accoutrements. The standardization of sizes in the Civil War allowed mass production of thousands of uniforms.

focused their efforts on provoking intervention by the governments of Europe, particularly those of Great Britain and France. General Robert E. Lee's two invasions of the North were undertaken with this goal in mind. The Confederates also hoped to create a sense of "war weariness" on the part of Lincoln's political opponents and the people of the North.

But ultimately, the war was not going to be resolved without the deployment of armies, navies, war command, and matériel. After Fort Sumter was bombarded, President Lincoln put out a call for volunteers to supplement the small number of regulars in the U.S. Army, Navy, and Marines. These had been diminished by those who left to fight for the South, including such high-ranking officers as Robert E. Lee, who resigned his officer's commission after his native state of Virginia left the Union. The Confederacy also established a small regular army, which mostly performed administrative functions. By the end of the war every state and territory in the Union had provided volunteer regiments or individual soldiers. All 11 seceding states provided volunteer forces to the Confederacy and the three Border States provided troops to both sides.

Tactically and logistically, the Civil War was different from the wars that came before it. The Civil War was the first large-scale conflict in which breech-loading rifles were used. Multi-shot repeating pistols, carbines, and rifles were all in use. The tactics of Europe's 19th-century wars, in which long lines of infantry faced each other and fired in volleys, were abandoned, as rifled muskets and the new conical Minié ball increased the accuracy and impact of infantry weapons. Technology greatly affected naval operations as well. The steam-powered navies featured ironclad ships, pivoting guns, electrically detonated mines, and a host of new vessels, including river rams, torpedo boats, and at least one submarine.

Logistically, the Civil War benefited from the industrial expansion of the era. Industrial technology increased the output and quality of weapons and matériel, while industrial inventions also had military uses. Railroads made the largest impact, dramatically improving the mobility of armies and better lines of supply. The field telegraph was also adopted as a command communications tool. Thaddeus Lowe and others developed aerial surveillance using gas balloons. The Confederacy employed commerce raiders on the high seas, while the North used marches through the South aimed at destroying supplies and industry, to affect the logistical capabilities of their enemy.

Finally, although the command structure of the armies on both sides incorporated organization by armies, corps, divisions, and brigades, the basic unit of both armies remained the regiment. In the most democratic society in the world at that time, the structure and command of the forces was conditioned by political as well as military necessity. Volunteer regiments elected their own company officers, while state governors appointed the field officers. Many generals, even those who had been professional soldiers before the war such as Ulysses S. Grant, received their appointments from state governors. The two opposing administrations were also forced to appoint a large number of inexperienced men to important commands simply because the constituencies that these political leaders represented were vital to the support of the war effort.

"It's just like shooting squirrels, only these squirrels have guns."

FEDERAL INSTRUCTOR TO NEW RECRUITS

CONFEDERATE UNIFORMS

The Confederacy had its own set of uniform regulations, much of which was adapted from the U.S. Army, but limits on supply required more improvisation in uniform styles. The standard color of Southern army, navy, and marine uniforms was Cadet Gray, but homespun cloth, often yellow-brown from butternut dye, was also used. As the war dragged on, soldiers in the field had to piece together uniforms, and many new recruits fought in their own clothes, with some regulation insignia, caps, or accoutrements.

ABOVE Northern 90-day volunteers parade in New York City on their way to war.

THE CONFEDERACY'S two great victories in Summer 1861, at First Manassas in July and Wilson's Creek in August, had not compelled the North into a truce. Instead, a great Union army amassed in the east, forcing the South to turn west and focus on the large front stretching from the Appalachian Mountains to the Mississippi River.

To take charge of this task the South called on Albert Sidney Johnston. Jefferson Davis, a West Point contemporary, made him a full general, the second highest-ranking officer in the Confederacy, but men and matériel were in short supply and little could be spared for the west.

Johnston approached this challenge with cleverness and enthusiasm. Identifying the important industrial and transportation city of Nashville, Tennessee, as the key, he formed a defensive line well north of it, in Kentucky. The thin line was anchored on the east by the Appalachians, on the west by Columbus, on cliffs above the Mississippi, with the center at Bowling Green. He ordered small cavalry raids and moved troops about with much fanfare to give the impression that his force was large and well armed.

For a while the ruse worked. William T. Sherman, in charge of the Department of Kentucky at Louisville, and later, Major General Henry W. Halleck, commanding the Department of Missouri from St. Louis, avoided attacking the Confederate line. One commander who was less convinced of the invincibility of Johnston and his Kentucky line was a recently appointed brigadier general, Ulysses S. Grant. Commanding a small department, he occupied the Kentucky riverport of Paducah, and challenged the Confederate position at Columbus under Leonidas Polk. His successes revealed a fighting spirit that Lincoln found intriguing.

Grant now turned his attention to the two strategic rivers close to Nashville: the Cumberland, which flowed through the city; and, west of it, the Tennessee. He and Flag Officer Andrew H. Foote lobbied for the opportunity to attack up the two rivers, using new ironclad river gunboats in combination with Grant's land force.

Johnston was gravely concerned. Of his two defensive forts situated on the river, Fort Henry, on low ground by the Tennessee, was virtually indefensible. Fort Donelson, on the Cumberland, was better sited, but also undermanned. On February 2, Grant set out with a force of 17,000 and seven of Foote's gunboats. On February 6, the gunboats opened fire on Fort Henry and it rapidly surrendered, allowing Grant to approach Fort Donelson from the land side. Grant arrived there on February 12, and was reinforced on the 14th by Foote, although the gunboat shelling was largely ineffective.

The next morning, the Confederates attacked Grant's right flank. Grant counterattacked, driving the Rebels back. That night, two of the three Confederate commanders, politicians John B. Floyd and Gideon Pillow, fled Fort Donelson, yielding the command to Brigadier General Simon S. Buckner. A unit under Lieutenant Colonel Nathan Bedford Forrest also escaped. On the 16th, Buckner requested a discussion of surrender terms with his pre-war friend Grant. "No terms

April 6 and 7, 1862

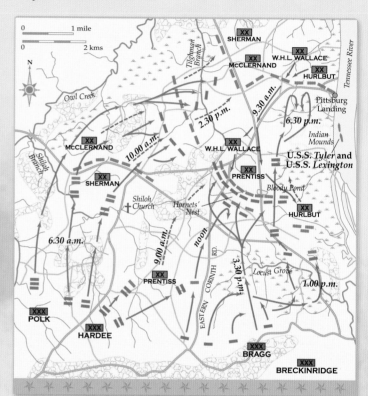

ABOVE On April 6, 1862, the camps of Maj. Gen. Ulysses S. Grant's soldiers at Pittsburg Landing were overrun by Confederates under Albert Sidney Johnston. As the morning attack wore on, Federal resistance stiffened, and Yankee soldiers in an area called the "Hornets' Nest" held off repeated assaults. A line of artillery on high ground and fire from two Federal gunboats halted the Rebel advance.

BACKGROUND The U.S. Navy gunboats *Tyler* and *Lexington* provided supporting fire for Federal troops at the Battle of Shiloh.

ULYSSES S. GRANT

Ulysses Simpson Grant was granted admission to West Point after his father doubted Grant's aptitude for the family tannery business. After graduating in 1843, Grant, an excellent horseman, was recognized for bravery in the Mexican War. He married Julia Dent and became a devoted family man, but struggled in peacetime military and civilian life. In 1861 he became commander of the 21st Illinois, gained a commission as a general of volunteers, and quickly found success in his true calling, military command.

LEFT Gen. Albert Sidney Johnston, CSA, was held in high regard in the Confederacy. But his promising leadership was cut short by a mortal wound received while directing an attack in Sarah Bell's Peach Orchard at Shiloh, April 6, 1862.

BELOW On April 6, at Shiloh, Federal soldiers from the divisions of W.H.L. Wallace and Benjamin Prentiss held against repeated attacks in an area dubbed the "Hornets' Nest" by Confederates, who were repulsed by thick rifle and cannon fire there.

await the arrival of the Army of the Ohio, under Brigadier General Don Carlos Buell.

Johnston and his commanders, reinforced by units from the Gulf Coast, decided to attack before Grant could be joined by Buell's men. At dawn on Sunday, April 6, the Union camps were overrun by nearly 40,000 charging, confident Southerners. But the troops camped around Shiloh Meeting House did not panic, giving ground only stubbornly under the inspired leadership of Sherman and Brigadier General Benjamin Prentiss.

Retreating Federals rallied along a farm track in an area soon to be known as the "Hornets' Nest". That afternoon, on another part of the battlefield, Johnston was mortally wounded. Beauregard called up artillery and drove the last Union soldiers from the Hornets' Nest after a seven-hour defense, but the Rebel offensive was losing steam. Grant set up a line of 53 artillery pieces on high ground, and with help from two timber-clad gunboats on the Tennessee, Confederate attack was checked.

The next morning, Beauregard prepared to resume the offensive, but Buell's force, and Grant's fresh division under Brigadier General Lew Wallace, began a counterattack that drove the Confederates back over the very ground they had taken the day before. Demoralized, the Southerners retreated to Corinth. With more than 24,000 casualties, neither side could mount a new attack immediately. Grant had had a close call, but his army survived to fight another day.

except an unconditional and immediate surrender will be accepted," Grant replied. That surrender accomplished, newspapers in the North lauded "Unconditional Surrender" Grant as a new hero.

Johnston abandoned Kentucky and Tennessee and fell back to northeastern Mississippi. Alarmed, Davis dispatched P.G.T. Beauregard to be Johnston's second-in-command. Grant pursued and put his army into camps at Pittsburg Landing to

THE WAR OUT WEST

AT THE BEGINNING of the Civil War, the Trans-Mississippi region west of the Mississippi River consisted of five states that remained loyal to the Union, three that seceded, Indian and organized territories, and the border state of Missouri. In the latter, sectional passions ran high well before the Civil War. As a result, Missouri experienced a large number of partisan skirmishes throughout the war. The organized armies in the state in 1861 were made up of Brigadier General Nathaniel Lyon's Federals, and the Missouri State Guards, a Rebel force trained by Major General Sterling Price.

In the summer of 1861, Lyon marched west from St. Louis in pursuit of the State Guards and Missouri's fleeing Confederate governor. He occupied Springfield in the southwest. Nearby, Price's Rebel group reinforced by units from Texas and elsewhere planned an attack on Lyon. Outnumbered, Lyon struck first, and early on August 10 he led his force into the Confederate camps, while Brigadier General Franz Sigel attempted to attack their flank. Initially successful, Sigel was driven back and Lyon was killed in an area later to be known as "Bloody Hill." The Federals withdrew beyond Springfield, leaving central Missouri under Confederate control.

In July, Lincoln sent Brigadier General John C. Frémont to stabilize Missouri, but the frontier explorer overstepped his political authority and was soon replaced. In early 1862, Brigadier General Samuel R. Curtis was assigned to drive Confederates from Missouri. Price withdrew to northwest Arkansas, where he was joined by forces under department commander Brigadier General Earl Van Dorn including 800 Native Americans.

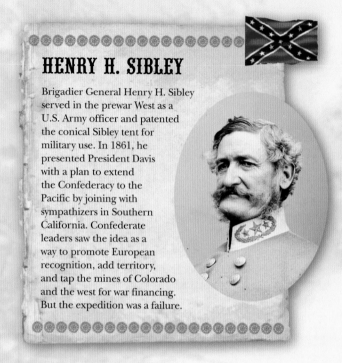

HENRY H. SIBLEY

Brigadier General Henry H. Sibley served in the prewar West as a U.S. Army officer and patented the conical Sibley tent for military use. In 1861, he presented President Davis with a plan to extend the Confederacy to the Pacific by joining with sympathizers in Southern California. Confederate leaders saw the idea as a way to promote European recognition, add territory, and tap the mines of Colorado and the west for war financing. But the expedition was a failure.

Curtis pushed into the Ozark Mountains of Arkansas, where, on March 7, at Pea Ridge, he was attacked by Van Dorn. Curtis and his smaller force resisted Rebel attacks on several fronts. The Confederates, short of ammunition, lost several high-ranking commanders. On March 8, they endured an artillery barrage and Federal counterattacks before retreating. Confederate units in the area then scattered, only regrouping when they were called east to meet the threat at Corinth, Mississippi. Combatants returned to the Boston Mountains in December, when the Confederates were again defeated, at the Battle of Prairie Grove.

ABOVE Maj. Gen. Frederick Steele, USA, was charged with cleaning the Rebels out of Arkansas after he took Little Rock in September 1863. But his expedition to Camden in the spring of 1864 was a disaster, and he narrowly escaped with his army after defeat at Jenkin's Ferry.

RIGHT Principal actions in the Trans-Mississippi. Although many of the engagements shown here were Confederate victories, key battles were won by the North and, coupled with control of the rivers and a steady Federal troop presence, the Rebels could not control the region.

BACKGROUND This fanciful lithograph depicts the March 7, 1862 attack on Federal forces by Missouri, Texas, and Native American Confederates in the Battle of Pea Ridge, called Elkhorn Tavern by the South.

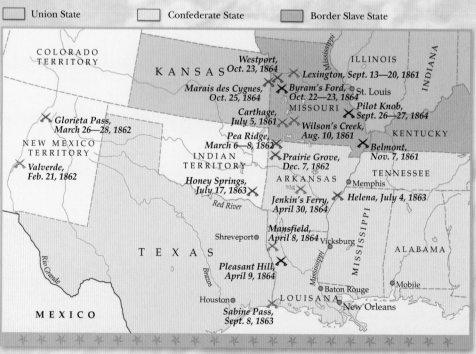

> *"He walked on, waving his sword and hallooing, and suddenly, blood appeared on the side of his head."*

FEDERAL OFFICER OBSERVING THE DEATH OF GENERAL LYON AT WILSON'S CREEK, AUG. 10, 1861

RIGHT This eyewitness painting depicts a series of wing dams, designed by engineering officer Joseph Bailey, that allowed Federal gunboats and transports to escape a rapidly falling Red River during the 1864 campaign.

BELOW The death of Brig. Gen. Nathaniel Lyon is shown in this period lithograph as he leads a Federal counterattack against the Rebels at "Bloody Hill" in the Battle of Wilson's Creek.

Farther west, Brigadier General Henry H. Sibley convinced President Davis to sanction an expedition into New Mexico. In late February 1862, his most irregular group of adventurous soldiers defeated a sizeable Federal force at Valverde, New Mexico, and then took Albuquerque and Santa Fe. But Colorado volunteers marched south to the defense of Fort Union in the northeast part of the territory. At the same time, the "California Column" began an eastward march to block Sibley's entry into that state.

On March 28, Federal soldiers surprised Sibley's Texans at Glorieta, along the Santa Fe Trail. The Confederate expedition was forced to fold due to lack of supplies after a group of Union soldiers destroyed their supply wagons. The return trip to Texas saw many Rebel lives lost to starvation and exposure.

For the next two and a half years, most of the action west of the Mississippi, except in Arkansas and Louisiana, consisted of isolated actions. Cavalry raids and guerrilla warfare continued. The Indian Territory and nearby border areas saw conflict between tribes loyal to the North and those who came under the influence of Confederate officers Douglas H. Cooper and Albert Pike. These former Indian agents rallied Native Americans to the cause of the

LEFT Brig. Gen. Albert Pike, CSA was a prewar scholar and lawyer, who successfully battled the Federal government in court on behalf of the Creek Nation. He was less able as a military commander, leading Native Americans to defeat in the Battle of Pea Ridge.

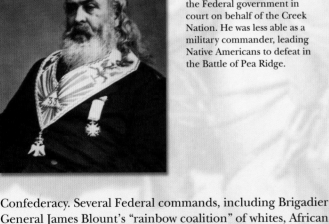

Confederacy. Several Federal commands, including Brigadier General James Blount's "rainbow coalition" of whites, African Americans, and Native Americans, fought them to maintain Union control of frontier areas.

The Federals also made several failed incursions into Texas. Then, in the autumn of 1864, Sterling Price again attempted to recover Missouri for the South. He led a force north from Arkansas toward St Louis, but a strong Federal presence forced him to change plans and head west. Price then suffered defeats at Independence and Westport and was hounded by three

Federal commands on a demoralizing retreat south.

After the North gained control of the Mississippi River, the Federals occupied Arkansas and Louisiana with little resistance, save for persistent small clashes with the command of Richard Taylor. Then in the spring of 1864, Taylor turned back a combined Union army and navy campaign up Louisiana's Red River, while the Federals also met with defeat at Camden in Arkansas. These failures meant the North had to keep large garrisons in the two states that could not be shifted to other theaters.

RIGHT Lt. Gen. Richard Taylor, CSA, the highly educated son of a U.S. President, learned military command with ease and, after serving under Stonewall Jackson, frustrated Federal efforts to take control of the Louisiana bayou country, the Red River, and Mobile.

THE WAR FOR THE MISSISSIPPI

February 1862 – July 1863

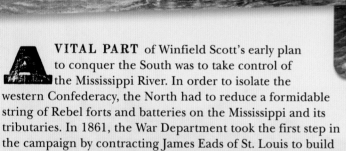

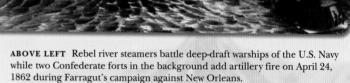

A **VITAL PART** of Winfield Scott's early plan to conquer the South was to take control of the Mississippi River. In order to isolate the western Confederacy, the North had to reduce a formidable string of Rebel forts and batteries on the Mississippi and its tributaries. In 1861, the War Department took the first step in the campaign by contracting James Eads of St. Louis to build seven river gunboats with iron-plated sides.

The gunboats took to the waterways in early 1862 under the command of Flag Officer Andrew H. Foote. After helping Major General Ulysses S. Grant secure Forts Henry and Donelson in February, Foote moved his gunboat navy to the Mississippi. The Confederates abandoned Columbus, Kentucky, so the Federals advanced to the next strong position, forts centered on Island No. 10 near New Madrid, Missouri. On April 4, the ironclad U.S.S. *Carondelet* ran the gauntlet of the island stronghold and three days later Major General John Pope's Army of the Mississippi engineered its way around three sides of Island No. 10, forcing the surrender of the 7,000-man Confederate garrison.

The next Union target was New Orleans, the South's largest city, well protected by virtually impassable swamps, and the Mississippi's current and shallows, which impeded deep-draft ships. The Confederates garrisoned Fort Jackson and Fort St. Philip, 50 miles below the city. Major General Mansfield Lovell with few troops available to him, had a few armed riverboats, and the Southerners were also building two large ironclads at New Orleans.

By March 1862, the Federal force was assembled in the Gulf of Mexico. Flag Officer David Glasgow Farragut was placed in charge of the expedition, while Commodore David D. Porter commanded a squadron of mortar schooners, and Major General Benjamin Butler's 18,000 soldiers were loaded onto transports. The Federal fleet maneuvered over the Southwest Pass bar and steamed up the Mississippi. The Confederates prepared the forts, and the unfinished ironclad C.S.S. *Louisiana* was towed upriver to act as a floating battery.

ABOVE LEFT Rebel river steamers battle deep-draft warships of the U.S. Navy while two Confederate forts in the background add artillery fire on April 24, 1862 during Farragut's campaign against New Orleans.

ABOVE Seven Federal ironclads and 11 mortar boats bombarded Confederate Island No. 10 in the Mississippi River for more than two weeks with little effect.

BELOW Major battles in the war for the Mississippi prior to Maj. Gen. U.S. Grant's 1863 Campaign against Vicksburg. The siege of Fort Hudson began during this campaign and ended after the surrender of Vicksburg.

> *"It was as if the artillery of heaven were playing upon Earth."*

FLAG OFFICER DAVID GLASGOW FARRAGUT ON RUNNING THE BATTERIES OF FORTS JACKSON AND ST. PHILIP

On April 18, Porter's 13-inch mortars began lobbing up to 2,000 shells a day toward the forts, with little visible effect. On April 20, Northern sailors cut a bulky chain strung across the river on ship hulks, allowing Farragut to run his ships past the forts.

On a moonless early morning, April 24, the column of 18 Federal ships started upriver, provoking furious fire from the forts.

The Rebel warships steamed downriver toward the action, and some vessels pushed flaming fire rafts at their Union opponents. The engagement lasted just two hours and all of Farragut's ships were able to get past the forts and steam toward New Orleans. Both of the large Confederate ironclads were blown up to prevent their capture. Cut off from New Orleans, the Rebel garrison surrendered on April 28.

In New Orleans, Lovell, his force reduced to 3,000, withdrew rather than risk destruction of the city by Farragut's powerful guns. On April 25, Farragut's ships arrived off the city and he demanded surrender from the city's officials, who refused. U.S. Marines then came ashore and occupied the city, which they then handed to the army. Butler, as military governor, exercised stern control of the city.

With New Orleans secure, Commodore James S. Palmer seized Baton Rouge, Louisiana, and Natchez, Mississippi. The race was on between two Federal naval forces converging on the South's bastion, Vicksburg.

Upriver, the Confederates built a fleet of new ram-equipped steamboats, which crippled Federal ironclads at Plum Point Bend, near Fort Pillow, 50 river miles

ABOVE AND BACKGROUND The deep-draft warships of Rear Admiral David G. Farragut's squadron run past the batteries of Port Hudson, Louisiana, on March 14, 1863.

north of Memphis. The North acquired its own fleet of rams, built and operated by Charles Ellet. On June 6, Ellet's rams scored a decisive victory over a small Confederate fleet at Memphis. The Stars and Stripes were then hoisted over the city.

The Memphis-based fleet now steamed downriver where, on July 1, it met Farragut, who had run the Vicksburg gauntlet on June 28. The sailors soon determined that with its sheer bluffs and well-placed batteries, Vicksburg could survive a naval bombardment and continue to harass free movement on the Mississippi. A 10,000-man force under Earl Van Dorn garrisoned Vicksburg, and the most successful Rebel ironclad, C.S.S. *Arkansas*, challenged Federal ships on the Mississippi and Yazoo Rivers. The meeting of the two Federal fleets at Vicksburg led some to conclude (falsely) that the river war was nearly over. Farragut's ships soon returned downriver and Vicksburg and Port Hudson would not be taken until land forces could aid naval action.

LEFT Rear Admiral David Dixon Porter, USN, was a pompous, yet innovative, naval officer, who worked well with Union generals Grant and Sherman.

SIEGE ARTILLERY

Coastal, river, and siege operations brought into play the Civil War's heavy artillery. The 8- and 10-inch Columbiads were the most popular smooth-bore guns, and the Rodman process made possible larger 12- and 15-inch models. The Rodmans were cast at Pittsburgh, while the rifled Parrott gun, in sizes up to 300-pounders, were cast at New York's West Point Foundry. The South made most of its heavy artillery at Richmond's Tredegar Iron Works, but imported a number of Blakely, Armstrong, and Whitworth rifled guns.

IN EARLY 1862, political pressure mounted on both Federal and Confederate commanders in the eastern theater for decisive action. The new Union General-in-Chief, Major General George B. McClellan, was urged to challenge General Joseph E. Johnston's Confederate army near Manassas Junction. On the Confederate side, Jefferson Davis, unhappy with Johnston's failure to exploit the victory at First Manassas, called on General Robert E. Lee to become his senior military advisor. Unwilling to meet Johnston head on, McClellan proposed landing the Army of the Potomac between Johnston's army and Richmond, Virginia. But Johnston withdrew behind the Rappahannock River, foiling the plan. McClellan then focused on the peninsula between the James and York Rivers, as an approach to Richmond while Davis and Lee formulated plans to deal with Federal forces throughout Virginia.

In March, the new Confederate commander in the Shenandoah Valley, Thomas J. "Stonewall" Jackson, attacked a division of Union soldiers at Kernstown. The battle sent a shock wave through Washington. Although defeated, Jackson was able to fashion one of the most brilliant campaigns of the war. Rapid marches enabled his "foot cavalry" to log 350 miles between April 30 and June 10. Jackson was able to occupy the attention of three Federal armies, including Major General Irvin McDowell's force, which was poised to move on Richmond from the north. "Old Jack" then left the valley after a Union trap in battles at Cross Keys and Port Republic. In continuing with the plan suggested by Lee, Jackson then marched to Richmond.

The Rebels, however, were still concerned over the landing of Federal soldiers at Fort Monroe in tidewater Virginia. When McDowell was ordered away from his southward march on Richmond to pursue Jackson, "Little Mac" became even more cautious and placed Yorktown under siege for several weeks, allowing an appreciative Johnston time to reinforce the peninsula.

April–July 1862

LEFT Maj. Gen. Thomas J. Jackson, CSA, led a brilliant campaign in the Shenandoah Valley in May and June of 1862 that caused the Peninsula Campaign of George McClellan to suffer, as three Federal armies were sent by the Washington leadership to pursue Jackson's "foot cavalry."

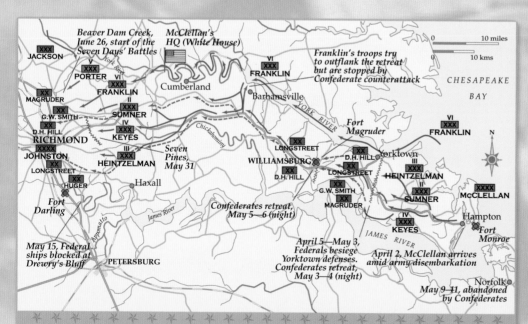

ABOVE This row of 13-inch seacoast mortars was a portion of the armament that Maj. Gen. George B. McClellan pressed into service for his siege against the thin Confederate line at Yorktown, April 5–May 3, 1862.

LEFT The Peninsula Campaign of the Army of the Potomac. After a slow start while besieging Yorktown, George McClellan then advanced his army with surprising speed over rain-swollen streams and muddy bogs to within sight of Richmond. Just when he had the Confederate capital in his sights, he paused again to assess the enemy, allowing first Gen. Joseph E. Johnston, unsuccessfully, then Robert E. Lee, successfully, to force a withdrawal and abandonment of the campaign.

Map labels: Beaver Dam Creek, June 26, start of the Seven Days' Battles · McClellan's HQ (White House) · JACKSON · PORTER · FRANKLIN · Cumberland · Franklin's troops try to outflank the retreat but are stopped by Confederate counterattack · CHESAPEAKE BAY · MAGRUDER · G.W. SMITH · SUMNER · Barhamsville · YORK RIVER · Fort Magruder · FRANKLIN · D.H. HILL · KEYES · RICHMOND · JOHNSTON · LONGSTREET · HEINTZELMAN · Seven Pines, May 31 · LONGSTREET · WILLIAMSBURG · D.H. HILL · Yorktown · HEINTZELMAN · Chickahominy · HUGER · Haxall · D.H. HILL · LONGSTREET · G.W. SMITH · MAGRUDER · SUMNER · MCCLELLAN · Fort Darling · Confederates retreat, May 5–6 (night) · James River · KEYES · Hampton · Fort Monroe · May 15, Federal ships blocked at Drewry's Bluff · PETERSBURG · Appomattox · April 5–May 3, Federals besiege Yorktown defenses. Confederates retreat, May 3–4 (night) · April 2, McClellan arrives amid army disembarkation · JAMES RIVER · Norfolk · May 9–11, abandoned by Confederates · 0 10 miles · 0 10 kms

LEFT In the final pursuit of Stonewall Jackson's army from the Shenandoah Valley, Federal forces close in on the Rebel camps at Cross Keys. On June 8, 1862, Brig. Gen. Richard Ewell held the ground against uncoordinated Union attacks. The Yanks' failure here led to a larger one the next day at Port Republic and Jackson slipped out of the valley with his force intact.

BACKGROUND Federal wagons take on supplies from rail cars at Savage's Station, Virginia, in the Peninsula Campaign. The needs of McClellan's 105,000-man army were daunting.

Johnston finally withdrew up the peninsula on May 3, his retreat protected by a delaying action by Major General James Longstreet at Williamsburg on May 5. Heavy rains, and disease in the swampy area, slowed McClellan's pursuit, but by the end of May the Army of the Potomac was within sight of Richmond. At the Battle of Seven Pines, or Fair Oaks, on May 31, a Rebel counter-offensive under Johnston was turned away by staunch Federal resistance, while Johnston was seriously wounded.

On June 1, Davis put Lee in command of the army, who then spent three and a half weeks strengthening the defenses of Richmond. He waited for the arrival of Jackson's army from the Shenandoah Valley, which together with six divisions at hand would make up the newly designated Army of Northern Virginia. At the same time, Major General J.E.B. Stuart began a reconnaissance of the Federal forces, a campaign that established the reputation of his cavalry corps.

On June 23, Lee conferred with his principal commanders, Longstreet, Major General A.P. Hill, Jackson, and Major General D.H. Hill. All units were to follow the lead of Jackson's force as he attempted to turn Major General Fitz John Porter's flank. On June 25, a skirmish at Oak Grove began the Seven Days' Battles. When Jackson's promised flanking move failed to materialize, the impulsive A.P. Hill started the attack against the Federals entrenched at Beaver Dam Creek, suffering a serious reversal.

Poor coordination of troop movements, Jackson's incapacity from stress fatigue, and gallant fighting by the North could have made the Seven Days' Battles a colossal defeat for Lee, but McClellan continued to overestimate the enemy's strength. He retreated to stronger positions, giving up ground to a numerically weaker foe. During the next five days, the South had only one tactical victory, at Gaines Mill, where an emerging general named John Bell Hood personally led a breakthrough attack.

Lee's gamble in the Seven Days' Battles resulted in 20,000 Confederate casualties. Yet McClellan insisted on withdrawing his army to Harrison's Landing, against the advice of his generals.

Lee was now able to reshape the Army of Northern Virginia into an efficient fighting force, with Jackson and Longstreet each leading a corps. Lee advanced rapidly north from Richmond, even as McClellan's army continued to evacuate the peninsula. Jackson defeated Nathaniel Banks at Cedar Mountain, and then turned to face the new Federal Army of Virginia, under Major General John Pope.

After initial skirmishes on August 28, Jackson took up a defensive position on the old Bull Run battlefield. Pope sent his army forward on the 29th, but bickering among the Federal commanders caused the attack to fail. The next day, Longstreet launched a hammer-like counterattack. The Federals withdrew late the same day and their stubborn resistance at Chantilly on September 1 thwarted Lee's plan to crush the force.

Although he could not destroy the Federal army in its Washington enclave, Lee readied for the invasion that he hoped would carry the war away from beleaguered Virginia. The war's momentum had returned to the South on all fronts, with significant political consequences.

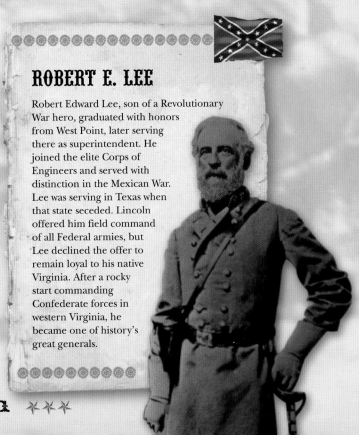

ROBERT E. LEE

Robert Edward Lee, son of a Revolutionary War hero, graduated with honors from West Point, later serving there as superintendent. He joined the elite Corps of Engineers and served with distinction in the Mexican War. Lee was serving in Texas when that state seceded. Lincoln offered him field command of all Federal armies, but Lee declined the offer to remain loyal to his native Virginia. After a rocky start commanding Confederate forces in western Virginia, he became one of history's great generals.

SPIES AND ESPIONAGE

THE CIVIL WAR has been called the first modern war. As well as assisting the military campaigns, technology also improved intelligence gathering, although most commanders relied on human espionage and analysis as their principal source of information for making combat decisions.

One of the North's most daring spies was a civilian, James J. Andrews. On the morning of April 12, 1862, in Northwest Georgia, Andrews and his accomplices seized a locomotive on the railroad that linked Chattanooga, Tennessee, with Atlanta. By burning bridges to cut off Chattanooga, Andrews's mission was to aid Federal troops advancing on the city from the west. At Big Shanty, Andrews and his raiders uncoupled the powerful locomotive *General* and several cars from a passenger train, and headed north with them toward Chattanooga.

The crew of the train, led by conductor William Fuller, gave pursuit in the southbound locomotive *Texas*, which they seized and ran in reverse. The raiders cut telegraph wires and attempted to slow their pursuers by placing obstacles on the track. The *General* exhausted its fuel near the Tennessee border

MILITARY TELEGRAPH

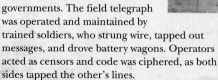

When the transcontinental telegraph was completed in 1861 the device was already an important military tool. The North established the U.S. Military Telegraph Service, beginning with control of lines around Washington, D.C. Both sides were able to exchange messages from within theaters of war and to their governments. The field telegraph was operated and maintained by trained soldiers, who strung wire, tapped out messages, and drove battery wagons. Operators acted as censors and code was ciphered, as both sides tapped the other's lines.

LEFT Pinkerton poses with Abraham Lincoln and Maj. Gen. John A. McClernand during the President's visit to Army of the Potomac headquarters in October 1862.

BELOW The locomotive *General* parked near Chattanooga after falling into Federal hands.

as the *Texas* closed in. The raiders fled into the Georgia hills, but were all captured within a week. Andrews and seven others were hanged, while the rest were imprisoned. A Southern newspaper described this "great locomotive chase" as "the deepest scheme that ever emanated from the brains of Yankees." It was an impressive example of the vulnerability of railroads to sabotage.

To no other campaign in the war was intelligence gathering more vital than to the 1862 Peninsula Campaign of Major General George B. McClellan. McClellan employed railroad security specialist Alan Pinkerton, who had planned Lincoln's secret route to his first inauguration in the face of threats on the President-elect's life. Pinkerton's intelligence was not an unqualified success—his agents were largely responsible for getting McClellan exaggerated estimates of enemy troop

strengths, encouraging McClellan's natural sense of caution. Pinkerton did, however, make many other valuable contributions to Union intelligence.

Thaddeus S.C. Lowe, a shrewd inventor, had sold lighter-than-air technology to Washington months before the Peninsula Campaign. Employing a portable gas generator of his own design, he launched his hydrogen balloon *Intrepid* and two others over the battle lines drawn before Richmond, providing McClellan with valuable reports of troop positions and movements. Rebel commanders, on the other hand, cursed the device as they tried to conceal their forces, but later launched a silk balloon of their own.

One of McClellan's most interesting operatives was a Canadian woman, Sarah Emma Edmonds, who had joined a Michigan regiment at the beginning of the war disguised as a man. In her male role, Sarah had served as a nurse, beginning at First Manassas. When her unit became part of the Army of the Potomac during the Peninsula Campaign, she volunteered for a reconnaissance operation. By her own account, Sarah quickly became one of McClellan's most reliable agents, frequently crossing enemy lines while donning a variety of disguises and bringing information valuable to the North with her.

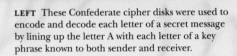

E. Porter Alexander, a brilliant Confederate officer who rose to be General Lee's Chief of Artillery, had developed the wigwag, or semaphore, system of flag communications with Albert J. Myers before the war. At First Manassas, Myers was a major with the Federal forces and Alexander was a captain on Brigadier General Beauregard's staff. Alexander used the wigwag signals to warn Rebel commanders of a potentially dangerous Union flanking move.

The reputation of Confederate spy Belle Boyd spread far and wide in 1862. Only 19 years old, Miss Boyd could be a demure Southern belle, or a sly vamp capable of coaxing vital information from smitten Yankee officers. She helped Stonewall Jackson track the Union forces in the Shenandoah Valley using information received from Federal officers who called on her.

Other Confederate spies operated in border areas such as Baltimore, where secessional sentiment was high. Baltimore dentist A.J. Volck acted as a Confederate courier and chronicled the events of the Civil War with satirical cartoons. Timothy Webster was an extremely effective Federal spy, going behind Southern lines and sending messages to Pinkerton. However, he was discovered in Richmond and hanged by the Rebels in April 1862.

Espionage continued in all theaters throughout the war. Spies infiltrated their enemy at many levels, even in the office of the U.S. Provost Marshall, the army's law-enforcement arm. Sometimes intelligence was easy to come by—Southern commanders got valuable intelligence by reading reports in Northern newspapers, as loose-lipped Federal officers leaked information to battlefield reporters.

RIGHT AND BACKGROUND Page six of a ten-page letter written to Jefferson Davis by Rose O'Neal Greenhow, while she was en route to Europe on a Confederate courier mission.

ROSE O'NEAL GREENHOW

Another famous Confederate spy was Washington socialite Rose O'Neal Greenhow. A widow when the war broke out, she had already befriended Presidents, members of the U.S. Congress, and military leaders. Her spy ring supplied information to Brigadier General P.G.T. Beauregard at First Manassas. Her exploits finally landed her in the Old Capitol Prison in Washington. Released and sent to Richmond, she later acted as a European diplomatic courier for President Davis. She died when the blockade runner on which she was a passenger sank in 1864.

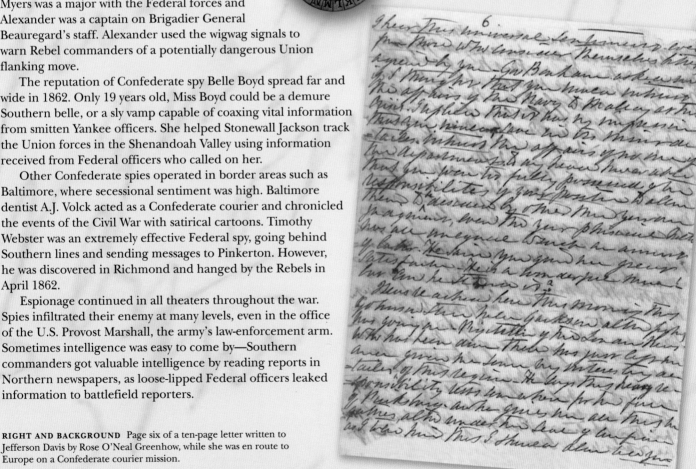

LEFT These Confederate cipher disks were used to encode and decode each letter of a secret message by lining up the letter A with each letter of a key phrase known to both sender and receiver.

AS THE MID-TERM Congressional elections in November of 1862 approached, Federal reverses in the summer and the stagnation of the Union advance on Corinth, Mississippi, lent weight to the assertions of the "Copperheads," the peace wing of the Democratic Party, that the only way to obtain peace was through an armistice. In this environment, the Rebels launched a two-prong attack to retake Kentucky.

General Braxton Bragg split his force in two, leaving 20,000 men under Sterling Price and Earl Van Dorn to move against Ulysses S. Grant in West Tennessee, while the rest of the force proceeded on a 776-mile train trip to Chattanooga, Tennessee. Major General Don Carlos Buell's Army of the Ohio was ordered to pursue Bragg.

Bragg departed Chattanooga for Kentucky on August 28. At the same time, Major General Edmund Kirby Smith's 18,000-man East Tennessee Army entered Kentucky from the east and defeated a Federal force at Richmond. Bragg, on entering Kentucky, issued a proclamation designed to swing the loyalty of its citizens to the Confederacy. It also appointed Richard Hawes as Confederate governor of the state, but his inauguration on October 4 was disrupted by enemy cannon fire. The action was a feint by Buell, who diverted his columns to Louisville, reorganized, and then set out after Bragg.

Buell took his army, reinforced to 60,000 men with two divisions from Grant, toward Bragg's main force at Bardstown. Major General Leonidas Polk, who was left in charge as Bragg went to Frankfort, was heavily outnumbered. He retreated to a defensive position just west of a Chaplin River tributary at Perryville, which provided a source of water for his troops in drought-stricken Kentucky. The need for water also drew a Federal corps to Perryville, which attacked Polk on the evening of October 7. Although the Rebels repulsed this foray, the Northerners returned the next morning under the rising leadership of Brigadier General Philip Sheridan.

September 1862– January 1863

On the morning of October 8, Sheridan gained control of the Perryville-Springfield Road creek crossing. Two of Buell's three corps joined Sheridan's force during the day. However, confusion reigned on both sides. Bragg, thinking the main Federal force was at Frankfort, ordered Polk to counter the Union advance. The Confederates had initial success against the green troops of Major General Alexander McCook, but reinforcements steadied the Federal line. Sheridan failed to get into the Rebels' rear, but turned back another Confederate attack later in the day.

BATTLE OF PERRYVILLE

Union—Army of the Ohio—Maj. Gen. Don Carlos Buell, commanding
Confederate—Army of Tennessee—Gen. Braxton Bragg, commanding, and Army of Kentucky—Maj. Gen. Edmund Kirby Smith, commanding

	UNION	CONFEDERATE
Total Engaged	36,940	16,000
Killed, Wounded and Captured	4,211	3,145

BATTLE OF STONES RIVER (MURFREESBORO)

Union—Army of the Cumberland—Maj. Gen. William S. Rosecrans, commanding
Confederate—Army of Tennessee—Gen. Braxton Bragg, commanding

	UNION	CONFEDERATE
Total Engaged	42,000	35,000
Killed	1,730	1,294
Wounded	7,802	7,945
Missing	3,717	1,027

LEFT Gen. Braxton Bragg, CSA, was a martinet who was almost universally disliked by officers and men who served under him. Despite a failure to sustain drives after initially gaining success, he continued in high command throughout the war because of his friendship with President Davis.

BACKGROUND Heavy fighting took place along this lane on the Perryville battlefield.

RIGHT Maj. Gen. Don Carlos Buell, USA, was a promising officer at the beginning of the war whose dour personality and caution led him to lose his army after Perryville.

When Buell ordered a resumption of the battle next morning, the Rebels were nowhere to be found. Bragg abandoned the campaign in the face of a larger army, short supplies, and lack of political support in Kentucky. Buell's pursuit of the smaller Rebel force of Bragg and Kirby Smith into East Tennessee was too cautious for Washington and on October 24 Lincoln removed him from command. Major General William S. Rosecrans was named to replace him and the army was redesignated as the Army of the Cumberland.

The winter of 1862, the winter of Fredericksburg and Chickasaw, was described by one Northern officer as "Our Valley Forge." One glimmer of hope did come in Middle Tennessee. On December 26, the 42,000-man Army of the Cumberland left Nashville. Although harassed by Bragg's cavalry division under Brigadier General Joseph Wheeler, the Federals under Rosecrans continued a steady march south. On December 29, they arrived two miles northwest of Murfreesboro to challenge Rebel positions astride Stones River. At daybreak on December 31, 13,000 Rebels tore into the Union right flank. In several hours of hard fighting, the Northern line was hurled back three miles. Once again, Philip Sheridan fought a skillful delaying action.

By noon, the hinge of the jack-knifed Union line was near a bend in Stones River known as Round Forest or Hell's Half Acre. Bragg ordered former United States Vice-President John C. Breckinridge to attack the position. The Rebels attacked piecemeal, suffering heavy casualties, but Bragg believed the Federals were withdrawing and prematurely telegraphed news of a great victory to Richmond.

After a lull on New Year's Day, Bragg ordered Breckinridge to take a Federal position east of Stones River. The Southerners were hammered by Federal artillery and a counterattack in the battle's final action. Unable to repulse the Army of the Cumberland, Bragg, on the night of January 3, 1863 retreated 40 miles south to Tullahoma. Little more than a stalemate, the Battle of Stones River, or Murfreesboro as the South called it, prompted a jubilant congratulatory telegraph message to Rosecrans from Lincoln.

POLITICAL WAR IN KENTUCKY AND TENNESSEE

The border state of Kentucky, at the geographical center of the divided nation, was nationalistic but had economic ties to the South. Initially, both sides respected its government's stated neutrality until the Confederates seized strategic points on the Mississippi River in September 1861. After the fall of Fort Donelson it remained in Union control, save for Braxton Bragg's brief failed campaign. Mountainous eastern Tennessee shared little with the rest of the state, and the North made control of the area a top priority.

PROCLAMATION.

To the Inhabitants of Kentucky!

Fellow Countrymen--

I HAVE KEPT MY PROMISE.

At the head of my old companions in arms, I am once more amongst you, with God's blessing no more to leave you.

Deprived as you are by these Northern Despots of all true information respecting the War, you are probably unaware that our holy Southern cause is everywhere in the ascendant.

The so-called "Young Napoleon," McClellan, has retreated from the Peninsula. Stonewall Jackson, the 'invincible,' is asserting the superiority of our Southern Banner against the armies of Pope, Banks, Fremont, Burnside, and that of McClellan, who has joined them. His ultimate success is assured.

NO POWER ON EARTH CAN MAKE US SLAVES!

Bragg, in Tennessee, is steadily advancing with an overwhelming force on Buel, who is retreating, whilst New Orleans is on the eve of being torn from the clutches of "Butler, the infamous," and restored to its legitimate and Confederate Government.

Kirby Smith at the head of a powerful army, is already in your State, whilst Forrest, Woodward, and myself have already proven to the Yankees our existance by taking Murfreesboro, Gallatin and Clarksville, burning the railroad bridges and damaging seriously the enemy.

AROUSE, KENTUCKIANS! shake off that listless feeling which was engendered by the presence of a powerful and relentless enemy. He is no longer to be feared! We have drawn his eye-teeth! there will soon be nothing left of him but his roar!

Let the old men of Kentucky, and our noble-hearted women, arm their sons and their lovers for the fight! Better death in our sacred cause than a life of slavery! Young men of Kentucky flock to my standard, it will always wave in the path of honor, and history will relate how you responded to my appeal, and how, by so doing, you saved your country!

JOHN H. MORGAN,

Aug. 22 1862 Col.-Commanding Brigade, C. S. A.

[MORGAN'S PRESS PRINT.]

LEFT In the Battle of Stones River or Murfreesboro, quick action by Rosecrans and his subordinates gave the North a victory in the difficult winter of 1862–63.

ANTIETAM

DOCUMENTS FLEW BACK AND FORTH across the English Channel in the summer of 1862 concerning recognition of the Confederacy. At stake for the Europeans was the gaining of a new diplomatic ally in the world order, and a continuous flow of cotton to the hungry mills of England and France, now disrupted by Lincoln's naval blockade of the South. In the case of France, there was also the hope of a close ally for that country's expansionist designs on Mexico. The victories of Robert E. Lee during that summer were the chief cause of this fevered buzz.

At the same time, across the Atlantic, Lincoln was preparing his own document, the Emancipation Proclamation, fulfilling his heartfelt desire to free the slaves in the states of the Confederacy. After reading the first draft to his cabinet, and on the advice of Secretary of State William Seward, he put it away, hoping to find military success to support his daring political stroke. The responsibility for achieving it was put in the hands

BELOW The Battle of Antietam was fought in three stages from north to south on divided terrain. The battle could have been decisive for the North had McClellan committed his ample reserves in a timely fashion, but he wavered and settled for possession of the battlefield after Lee's withdrawal.

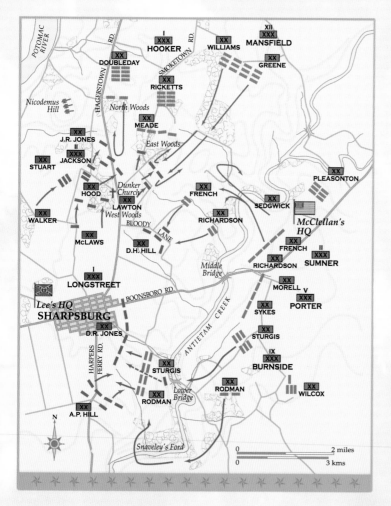

September 17, 1862

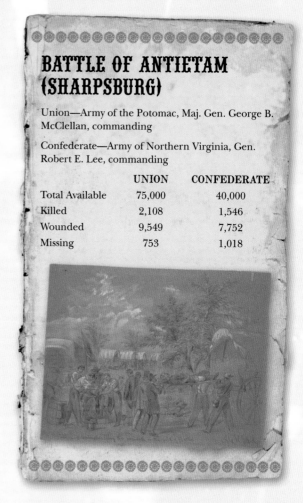

BATTLE OF ANTIETAM (SHARPSBURG)

Union—Army of the Potomac, Maj. Gen. George B. McClellan, commanding

Confederate—Army of Northern Virginia, Gen. Robert E. Lee, commanding

	UNION	CONFEDERATE
Total Available	75,000	40,000
Killed	2,108	1,546
Wounded	9,549	7,752
Missing	753	1,018

of the general who had lost spectacularly to Lee earlier in the year, George B. McClellan. In the late summer of 1862, Lincoln restored McClellan's command of the mammoth Army of the Potomac, having found no better leader for it.

As McClellan marched his soldiers across western Maryland in pursuit of Lee's army, he had no idea how the future of one of America's greatest documents would be affected by the chance finding of another document. Federal soldiers inspecting an abandoned Rebel camp near Frederick, Maryland, discovered three cigars wrapped in a copy of Lee's Special Order No. 191, his plan for the disposition of his troops for the capture of Harpers Ferry, a prime objective on his march north. Lee did capture Harpers Ferry, and its large Federal garrison with part of Thomas "Stonewall" Jackson's Corps, but McClellan, armed with his new-found knowledge, pressed west against Lee's main force.

On September 14, 1862, at South Mountain, Maryland, the VI and IX Corps of the Army of the

ABOVE Federal infantry advance toward Dunker Church, the location of Rebel artillery and an objective of the early morning fighting that raged in a cornfield, surrounded by woods on three sides.

Potomac challenged James Longstreet's Corps, which Lee had sent to delay the Yanks until he could reunite his army with Jackson's force. Although the Confederates withdrew that night after heavy fighting, Lee's delaying action had bought a day. When McClellan arrived in front of Lee's prepared position behind Antietam Creek on September 15, the Union commander did not engage the enemy immediately, even though the Rebel force was still consolidating.

McClellan's simple battle plan, attack first Lee's left, then his right, and then exploit any success gained with a follow-up punch to the center, was hampered by what the Prussian military philosopher Karl Von Clausowitz described as "battlefield friction." The attack, begun in the pre-dawn hours of September 17, did not go as planned. Jackson's Corps turned back assaults by men under Joseph Hooker and Joseph Mansfield on the northern part of the battlefield near the Dunker Church. In the south, Burnside's men could not initially locate the fordable portions of Antietam Creek and were pinned down at a stone bridge. Although the Federal II Corps drove D.H. Hill's men from the sunken road in the center, the fractured terrain and lack of communication worked in Lee's favor and against McClellan. Lee shifted men from other parts of the battlefield and turned back the Federal advance in the center.

McClellan's force achieved a breakthrough in the late afternoon when Burnside's men stormed across the stone bridge. But a force under A.P. Hill, after a hard march from Harpers Ferry, turned back Burnside's advance. Even though McClellan had more fresh troops available the next day than Lee had in his entire army, he did not continue to drive Lee's troops into the Potomac. Lee made that decision himself, withdrawing across the river into Virginia in the face of a reorganized Federal army. McClellan's claim of a great victory achieved was overstated, and his failure to pursue and destroy Lee eventually cost him his job. It was, however, enough of a success for Lincoln to pull the Emancipation Proclamation out of the drawer, make a few revisions, and announce it to the world on September 22, 1862.

LEFT Confederate dead in Bloody Lane, photographed by Alexander Gardner. This and other photographs of the battle brought the horror of war to a curious public when first exhibited in Matthew Brady's New York gallery in October 1862.

BACKGROUND Federal infantry protects the battery of Capt. Stephen H. Weed, attached to the Army of the Potomac V Corps, at Antietam.

December 13, 1862

Falmouth

11.00 a.m.–5.00 p.m. repeated attacks

Dec. 11, Federals cross river in boats to drive off snipers

STAFFORD

SUMNER XXX

COUCH XXX II

BUTTERFIELD XXX V

BURNSIDE XXXX

ANDERSON XX

MARYE'S HEIGHTS

PLANK RD.

FREDERICKSBURG

RANSOM XX

PICKETT XX

Hazel Run

HEIGHTS

WILCOX IX XXX

HOOKER XXX

pontoon bridges

McLAWS XX

LONGSTREET XXX

W.F. SMITH VI XXX

FRANKLIN XXX

Deep Run

TELEGRAPH RD.

Rappahannock

10.00–11.00 a.m.

HOOD XX

1.30 p.m.

REYNOLDS XXX I

A.P. HILL XX

1.00 p.m. *noon*

LEE XXXX

N

TALIAFERRO XX

D.H. HILL XX

STUART XX

EARLY XX

2.15 p.m., counterattack

JACKSON XXX II

0 — 1 mile
0 — 1 km

ABOVE The battlefield at Fredericksburg. Federal infantry crossed the river with artillery support that was well-sited on Stafford Heights. But they were unable to penetrate the prepared line the Confederates held on the hills behind Fredericksburg. When a breakthrough was achieved in front of Stonewall Jackson's II Corps, hesitation by the Union leadership allowed the opportunity to slip away.

RIGHT Maj. Gen. Ambrose E. Burnside did not feel qualified to lead the Army of the Potomac in late 1862. It is said Burnside only took the job to prevent his rival, Maj. Gen. Joseph Hooker, from getting it.

BELOW Burnside attempted a flanking move on Lee's line at Banks' Ford beginning on January 19, 1863. But nature interfered before the Rebels had to—rain, sleet, and high winds forced the so-called "Mud March" to be canceled within a few days.

AFTER DRIVING the Army of Northern Virginia from Maryland at the Battle of Antietam, Major General George B. McClellan spent the next weeks resting and refitting his army. Abraham Lincoln visited McClellan in October and urged him to move while the roads were still good and before Robert E. Lee's command was again battle-ready. The President's words fell on deaf ears. Northern newspapers and members of Congress began to call for McClellan's removal, but Lincoln resisted.

McClellan finally moved his army across the Potomac, beginning on October 26, but so slowly that Lee was able to send Longstreet's Corps into Culpeper County, Virginia, while Stonewall Jackson remained in the Shenandoah Valley on the Union flank. Meanwhile, on October 25, Major General J.E.B. Stuart's cavalry raided Chambersburg, Pennsylvania, adding to the trepidation in Washington. The President could wait no longer. On November 7, Lincoln removed McClellan from command and appointed Major General Ambrose Burnside in his place.

Fredericksburg was the principal city between Washington and the Confederate capital. By November 17, Burnside had rapidly moved his force to Falmouth, across the Rappahannock River from the city. The move concerned Lee, who had only a few troops in the area.

But the Rebels had destroyed all the bridges over the Rappahannock, so Burnside had to rely on pontoon bridges to effect a crossing. Due to poor planning and obstacles on the route, the bridges did not arrive until late November. By this time Lee had most of his 75,000 veterans in Fredericksburg. Unable to bridge the river as he had wanted, and with the Army of Northern Virginia at his front, and under political pressure for an offensive, Burnside modified his strategy.

The Army of the Potomac was reorganized into three grand divisions. The Right Grand Division, under Major General Edwin

> *"My heart bleeds at the death of every one of our gallant men."*
>
> GENERAL LEE TO HIS WIFE ON CONFEDERATE
> LOSSES AT FREDERICKSBURG

Sumner, arrived first at the Rappahannock, but heavy rains kept his troops from crossing the river. The Left Grand Division was under the command of Major General William B. Franklin, while Major General Joseph Hooker commanded the Center Grand Division. Even after the arrival of the pontoon boats, Burnside spent another two weeks deciding what to do.

ABOVE Federal engineers lay a pontoon bridge over the Rappahannock River as Confederate snipers fire on them from Fredericksburg. Despite this, the engineers got the job done.

LEFT AND BACKGROUND This photograph shows a portion of the open field that Maj. Gen. Edwin V. Sumner's Grand Division had to cross in front of a devastating fire from the Confederate I Corps.

Seeking to surprise the enemy by hitting him head-on, Burnside elected to cross the river at Fredericksburg, even though the Rebels had several weeks to strengthen their defensive position. On December 11, Federal engineers began the difficult task of laying the six bridges. At the crossing site in Fredericksburg, the operation was attempted even under deadly fire from Southern sharpshooters. A two-hour Union artillery barrage from Stafford Heights failed to dislodge the snipers.

Finally, Burnside sent infantry across the river in pontoon boats and they drove the Rebels from town. Late on the 11th, Union troops crossed the bridges and occupied Fredericksburg, with more troops crossing the following day. South of town, the men of Franklin's Grand Division faced Jackson's Corps near Hamilton's Crossing. On the high ground west and upstream

from town, Longstreet's Corps occupied Marye's and Willis Heights. Below the heights, Cobb's reinforced brigade stood protected behind a stone wall. Broad fields separated the Confederate positions from the Federals forming in town.

Around 10.00 a.m. on December 13, a heavy curtain of fog suddenly lifted, and south of Fredericksburg, Franklin's Grand Division, supported by part of Hooker's, advanced on the Rebel right. A division of Pennsylvanians under Major General George G. Meade discovered a seam in Jackson's line and stormed ahead. But Burnside's unclear instructions to Franklin endangered the best opportunity for a breakthrough. The Rebels closed the gap and turned back Meade's advance.

In Fredericksburg, the Federals were faring less well. The Right Grand Division, joined by several of Hooker's divisions, advanced up sloping fields, their progress slowed by fences, orchards, houses, and a drainage canal; they charged, but never reached the Georgians and North Carolinians, who fired their rifled muskets so rapidly as to achieve a machine-gun-like effect. Longstreet later wrote, "I thought, as I saw the Federals come again and again to their death, that they deserved success if courage and daring could entitle soldiers to victory."

The short December day drew a curtain of twilight over the carnage after six charges. Burnside assumed full responsibility. He planned a desperate assault the next day, intending to personally lead his former command, the IX Corps, but subordinates convinced him to abandon the idea.

After only light skirmishing, the Federals withdrew back across the river on the night of December 15. The disaster of Fredericksburg caused a temporary political division in Lincoln's cabinet, which the President quickly repaired. Burnside failed to control his dissenters, especially Hooker and Franklin, who openly disagreed with him over a plan to turn Lee's left flank by fording the Rappahannock north of Fredericksburg. Heavy rains, sleet, and snow inundated this so-called "Mud March," which was finally abandoned on January 24.

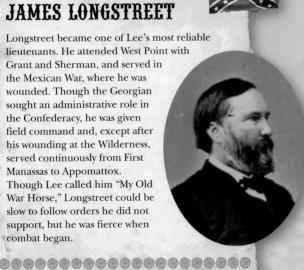

JAMES LONGSTREET

Longstreet became one of Lee's most reliable lieutenants. He attended West Point with Grant and Sherman, and served in the Mexican War, where he was wounded. Though the Georgian sought an administrative role in the Confederacy, he was given field command and, except after his wounding at the Wilderness, served continuously from First Manassas to Appomattox. Though Lee called him "My Old War Horse," Longstreet could be slow to follow orders he did not support, but he was fierce when combat began.

BATTLE OF CHANCELLORSVILLE

May 2 and 3, 1863

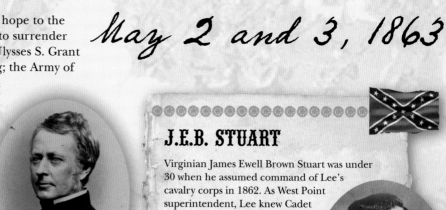

THE SPRING OF 1863 brought new hope to the North that the South might be forced to surrender before the war entered its third year: Ulysses S. Grant started a new and promising drive on Vicksburg; the Army of the Cumberland readied for its next advance in Middle Tennessee; and in the east, the Army of the Potomac had another new commander, as President Lincoln had replaced Ambrose Burnside with Major General Joseph Hooker shortly after the "Mud March."

Lincoln made the appointment with some reservation because of Hooker's reputation for intrigue and rowdiness. But Hooker was a popular choice with the men. He improved conditions in the camps and hospitals; rid the army of corrupt quartermasters; and created an esprit de corps, with distinctive badges for each corps. A soldier in the ranks wrote, "Under Hooker, we began to live."

BELOW In the Battle of Chancellorsville Robert E. Lee divided his army in the face of a larger enemy, and he counted on the uncoordinated efforts of the Army of the Potomac commanders to allow him to defeat their army in detail. He was not disappointed here, as Federal caution played right into his plan.

ABOVE Maj. Gen. Joseph Hooker was an officer known for personal bravery, but also for intrigue. He proved to be a capable subordinate, but good judgment gave way to caution and uncertainty when he was given overall command.

J.E.B. STUART

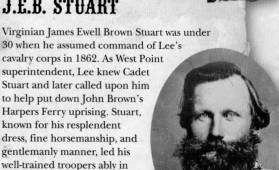

Virginian James Ewell Brown Stuart was under 30 when he assumed command of Lee's cavalry corps in 1862. As West Point superintendent, Lee knew Cadet Stuart and later called upon him to help put down John Brown's Harpers Ferry uprising. Stuart, known for his resplendent dress, fine horsemanship, and gentlemanly manner, led his well-trained troopers ably in reconnaissance and combat missions from First Manassas to his death at Yellow Tavern in May 1864. He was a commander respected by Southerners and Northerners alike.

The increasing strength of the Army of the Potomac concerned Robert E. Lee, who had recently cut his own troop strength by sending James Longstreet and two divisions to confront a Union threat developing around tidewater Virginia. Lee's men held the heights behind Fredericksburg and had a 10-mile network of trenches along the Rappahannock.

The reorganized Federal cavalry corps, 10,000 strong, crossed the Rappahannock on April 27, and headed south to cut Lee's supply lines and distract the Rebel cavalry. Hooker ordered Major General John Sedgwick's reinforced VI Corps at Fredericksburg to feign an attack to keep Lee occupied. He then marched 45,000 men swiftly around Lee's left flank and by the evening of April 30, most of this force was concentrated around a crossroads called Chancellorsville.

Lee guessed correctly that the main Federal threat would come there. He left 10,000 men at Fredericksburg under Major General Jubal Early, and marched the rest of his army toward Chancellorsville. On May 1, they clashed with some of Hooker's force east of crossroads. Hooker failed to exploit his advantage, ordering his men back to a defensive position in the dense thicket around Chancellorsville known locally as the Wilderness.

Map:
- Ely's Ford
- F. LEE
- Rapidan River
- U.S. Ford
- *May 5 (night), Hooker retreats across river*
- *May 2, 5.15 p.m., Jackson routs Federals with surprise attack*
- STUART
- JACKSON
- REYNOLDS
- HOOKER
- Rappahannock
- *May 2, 9.30 p.m., Jackson accidentally shot dead by Confederate picket. Command passes to Stuart*
- THE WILDERNESS
- MEADE
- SLOCUM
- A.P. HILL
- SICKLES
- HOWARD
- RODES
- HOWARD
- COUCH
- *May 3 (early morning), Hooker's entire force retreats*
- COLSTON
- PLANK RD.
- STUART
- HETH
- SLOCUM
- Chancellorsville
- Mott's Run
- ORANGE
- HETH
- McLAWS
- OLD ORANGE PIKE
- BROCK RD.
- SICKLES
- ANDERSON
- LEE
- Catherine Furnace
- PLANK RD.
- *May 3–4, Lee countermarches against Sedgwick's advance from Fredericksburg, allowing Hooker to evacuate north on May 5 (night)*
- Lewis Creek
- *May 2, 7.00 a.m.–5.00 p.m., Jackson marches around Hooker, while Lee keeps pressure on Federals*
- 2 miles
- 2 kms

> *"Let us cross over the river, and rest under the shade of the trees."*

GENERAL "STONEWALL" JACKSON'S LAST WORDS

Lee now made a daring move by splitting his army. He sent the bulk of his force under Stonewall Jackson on a roundabout 12-mile march through the Wilderness early on May 2. Lee was left with just 15,000 men to challenge Hooker's more than 40,000, while Early faced almost three-to-one odds in Fredericksburg. Although Major General Daniel Sickles's III Corps discovered Jackson's column on May 2, Hooker chose to interpret this as a Confederate retreat to the southwest. So that evening, the soldiers of Major General Oliver O. Howard's XI Corps were ill-prepared for the grayclad thunderbolt coming from the west.

Jackson's men rolled up the Union flank and pushed the battle east, to the vicinity of the Chancellorsville mansion. But the Union line steadied and the Confederates were exhausted after their all-night march. The fight continued after dark, but the Rebel advance was stopped. That night, as General Jackson was reconnoitering the Wilderness, Confederate pickets mistook him for a Union soldier and shot him. He was taken behind the lines, where his left arm was amputated. Eight days later, he died of pneumonia at Guinea Station.

On May 3, the disheartened Rebels engaged in some of the hardest fighting of the war. Hooker had already ordered Sedgwick forward the previous day; the VI Corps had taken the heights at Fredericksburg and was pushing toward Lee's rear at Salem Church. Reinforced, Hooker had a two-to-one advantage over Lee by May 3, but he pulled back to a tighter defensive position. On that day Hooker was stunned when a cannon ball splintered a wooden post near where he was standing. On the night of May 5, against the wishes of his corps commanders, Hooker ordered the Army of the Potomac back across the

SPENCER CARBINE

The Spencer repeating carbine, like other Civil War carbines, was distinguished by a sliding bar and ring to secure the weapon while riding on horseback. The Spencer had a magazine tube in the stock that was loaded with seven rimfire cartridges. Cocking the hammer and pulling a loading lever popped a cartridge into the chamber, which was then struck by a side hammer. Most of the 200,000 carbines produced in the war were used by the North, giving them a combat advantage.

Rappahannock. "Fighting Joe" Hooker had the fight knocked out of him.

Though saddened by the loss of his most trusted subordinate, Robert E. Lee was pleased with the Army of Northern Virginia's domination in the Battle of Chancellorsville. This important victory also took the war away from the Virginia Piedmont for a time and gave Lee the confidence to go on the offensive.

BACKGROUND General Robert E. Lee achieved his greatest victory of the Civil War at Chancellorsville, though at a terrible cost, as Stonewall Jackson received a fatal wound and Maj. Gen. A. P. Hill was wounded as well.

BELOW LEFT Lt. Gen. Thomas J. "Stonewall" Jackson had many curious personal habits, particularly regarding his health and religion. However, he was a devoted family man and a wonderful leader of men, stern but commanding respect. As a tactician, he had few equals in the Civil War and his methods signaled the future of military leadership.

BELOW Confederate dead at the stone wall in Fredericksburg after the assault by the Federal VI Corps in the Battle of Chancellorsville. The same stone wall that had been such an ally in the Battle of Fredericksburg proved to be vulnerable when held by Jubal Early's thin ranks on May 3, 1863.

CAVALRY

THOUGH THE CONTRIBUTIONS of mounted forces in the Civil War were significant, they could not stand on their own—without the presence of the foot soldiers, no victory on the battlefield could turn the fortunes of war. Yet, the romantic allure of a Civil War cavalry charge created larger-than-life heroes.

The cavalry missions of the Civil War differed from those of earlier 18th- and 19th-century wars, as technology modified the roles of mounted troops. The experience of many officers and enlisted men, who, as members of U.S. Army cavalry units, had participated in pre-war actions against western tribes of Native Americans, brought an understanding of the kind of combat that would occur in many Civil War confrontations. Able to operate while mounted and also dismounted as riflemen, the mobility and quickness of the cavalry would act as a vital adjunct to many campaigns and create stand-alone victories as well.

Cavalry performed a range of tactical functions. First, the mounted troopers could reconnoiter enemy units and positions. The cavalry also acted as skirmishers, engaging the

LEFT Maj. Gen. J.E.B. Stuart at the head of his column. Although he enjoyed the pomp and attention his position afforded him, Stuart was also a deeply religious man who neither swore nor drank.

"THE WIZARD OF THE SADDLE"—NATHAN BEDFORD FORREST

Forrest was a commander both feared and respected by his enemies. He rose from poverty to become a successful Tennessee planter and slave trader, then joined the Confederate army as a private. Lacking formal military training, his self-reliance enabled him to grasp strategy and tactics. A skillful cavalry leader, he led his mounted strike force behind enemy lines on raids against railroads and isolated garrisons and fought head-to-head battles when challenged.

the enemy; or simply acted as an irritant by drawing opposing forces away from principal campaigns.

At the beginning of the war, the Confederate army particularly excelled in cavalry operations. Many men of the Southern gentry class had spent time in the saddle and possessed superior riding skills. Volunteer units of Federal cavalry were not formed immediately. U.S. regulars provided six regiments in the Federal army and served in the initial actions. But the need for more cavalry prompted the enlistment and equipping of volunteer Union cavalry regiments, though it was only in the summer

enemy while screening the movements of the rest of the army. They could also advance quickly and hold positions until infantry units secured them, and cover withdrawals or act as escorts for artillery and slow-moving wagon trains. They could also fill in gaps in lines until infantry units could be moved into position.

Cavalry also had a strategic role as independent units, especially as raiders. The most effective of these was the Confederacy's Nathan Bedford Forrest, but both sides had cavalry units that acted as independent components for varying lengths of time. Raiders engaged in acts of sabotage, especially against railroad operations; terrorized towns and garrisons to exact ransom, gain supplies, or inflict psychological damage on

CAVALRY SABER

The cavalry saber was carried by most troopers and officers throughout the war, even though its combat use was diminishing as the role of cavalry expanded and firearms became standard weapons for mounted soldiers. The U.S. Model 1840 cavalry saber and Model 1860 light cavalry saber both had curved blades, brass guards, and steel scabbards. Sabers were still valuable in boot-to-boot mounted clashes such as those at Brandy Station and Gettysburg.

RIGHT Cavalry troopers raid an enemy wagon train in this dramatic woodcut. Destruction of supplies and means of transportation was a principal strategic use of cavalry.

BACKGROUND Horse artillery units of the Federal Army of the Potomac stand ready to march. The light howitzers and rifles of the cavalry provided support to mounted and dragoon operations and could threaten enemy facilities on raids. The Confederacy's Nathan Bedford Forrest used his cannons quite effectively on a number of raids against Northern depots.

of 1863 that Federal cavalry began to operate on an equal footing with the Southern horsemen.

One of the most effective cavalry leaders of the Civil War was J.E.B. Stuart. He led the cavalry corps of General Robert E. Lee's Army of Northern Virginia. Stuart led his command on reconnaissance missions and raids in the first year of Lee's leadership with very little interference from the Federal cavalry. After Major General Joseph Hooker created a separate cavalry corps in the Army of the Potomac, a group of Northern cavalry commanders emerged to challenge Stuart's elite horsemen.

LEFT Colonel John S. Mosby, CSA, began the Civil War at First Manassas and served under Stuart, but then formed a well-disciplined unit under the partisan Ranger Law and upset numerous Federal operations throughout Northern Virginia.

RIGHT Lt. George Armstrong Custer, USA, last in the West Point Class of '61, pictured with his friend and mascot during the Peninsula Campaign. Rising quickly to general in 1863, he was an intrepid cavalry leader who achieved great success in the Gettysburg Campaign and beyond.

As the Army of Northern Virginia was advancing in June of 1863 for Lee's second invasion of the North, an action took place between cavalry forces in Culpeper County, Virginia. Most cavalry combat in the Civil War was fought in the style of dragoons: troopers would ride to a location, dismount, and fire their weapons while on the ground. The Battle of Brandy Station on June 9 was a more traditional clash, complete with saber charges and hand-to-hand combat on horseback. The hours-long battle ranged over several fronts across rolling pastures and Robert E. Lee reportedly "expressed great admiration of [the] grit and courage manifested by soldiers on both sides."

The Federal troopers had now reached a high level of combat skill. In the ensuing actions at Gettysburg, Stuart's cavalry was sufficiently challenged to affect the outcome of the battle. Union cavalry commanders, including George Armstrong Custer, David Gregg, and Wesley Merritt, now began to score victories. When Major General Philip H. Sheridan came east to head the Army of the Potomac's cavalry corps in 1864, he used these commanders to create a superior fighting force that had a significant impact in subsequent major campaigns.

In the Western theater, the cavalry of Forrest, Brigadier General John Hunt Morgan, and Brigadier General Joseph Wheeler gave the South an edge in mounted operations. In the Mississippi basin, John Shelby and John S. Marmaduke also scored victories in raids and skirmishes with Federal forces. Slowly, a few Federal leaders, including Benjamin Grierson and James H. Wilson, began to lead a determined group of Union troopers in tactical and strategic operations that would positively impact Union operations in the west.

GETTYSBURG—CAMPAIGN AT A CROSSROADS

AFTER THE BATTLE of Chancellorsville, General Robert E. Lee was confident that a renewed invasion of the North would achieve his political and military goals. On June 3, 1863, Lee began redeploying his army northwest over the route used earlier by his fallen comrade, Stonewall Jackson. Of Jackson, Lee said after Chancellorsville, "I know not how to replace him."

Lee named Lieutenant General Richard Ewell to take Jackson's place. A new III Corps was formed under Lieutenant General A. P. Hill, to join Ewell's II Corps and Lieutenant General James Longstreet's I Corps. Lee instructed Major General J.E.B. Stuart to keep the cavalry in advance and to shadow the Army of the Potomac. Stuart interpreted this vague order as giving him carte blanche to battle Federal horsemen and raid Northern supply trains.

Major General Joseph Hooker held his forces near Fredericksburg. He then dispatched the Federal cavalry corps under Major General Alfred Pleasanton to investigate Confederate cavalry movements. When Pleasanton discovered Stuart in Culpeper County, Virginia, the largest mounted battle ever fought in the western hemisphere took place on June 9 at Brandy Station.

July 1 and 2, 1863

LEFT Maj. Gen. George G. Meade, USA, was the son of an agent for the U.S. Navy, but the military was not his first career choice. However, after attending West Point and serving in the Mexican War, he became a noted U.S. Army engineer. He served with distinction in the major campaigns of the Army of the Potomac and reluctantly agreed to head the force after his superior, Maj. Gen. John F. Reynolds, turned down the job.

LEFT The situation at Gettysburg on July 2, 1863. Robert E. Lee was correct in instructing his two senior corps commanders to assault the flanks of the Federal line because units of the Army of the Potomac were still arriving on the field. But while A.P. Hill held the center, James Longstreet and Richard Ewell took most of the day preparing their attacks. Through good fortune, timely management, and a determined fighting force, Federal leaders were able to turn back each of the July 2 Confederate offensives.

The two cavalry forces battled on in Virginia's Loudoun Valley while the Confederate infantry marched north, followed by the Army of the Potomac. Hooker resigned his command after a disagreement with Washington over obtaining the soldiers of the Harpers Ferry garrison, which shortly thereafter surrendered to Ewell's Rebels. On June 28, he was replaced by Major General George Gordon Meade.

Stuart began another of his famous rides around the Union army on June 27. He fell out of touch with the advancing infantry columns and only reunited with Lee after the Battle of Gettysburg had begun. When Lee learned that 90,000 Federals were concentrated between his scattered army and Washington, he decided to place his army at Cashtown, Pennsylvania. Meade began to form a defense line along Big Pipe Creek, near Maryland's northern border, while the Federal cavalry under Brigadier General John Buford took up positions west of Gettysburg, a small farm town where nine roads converged.

On the morning of July 1, 1863, Buford's dismounted troopers clashed with Major General Henry Heth's infantry, advancing south from Cashtown in search of shoes at Gettysburg. The skirmish quickly escalated into a general engagement as more soldiers from Hill's Corps clashed with infantry from the Federal I Corps. Though these soldiers held Oak Ridge, units of Major General O.O. Howard's XI Corps arrived and failed to close a gap to meet the right of the I Corps. Units of Ewell's Rebel corps under Major General Robert Rodes arrived to exploit that gap.

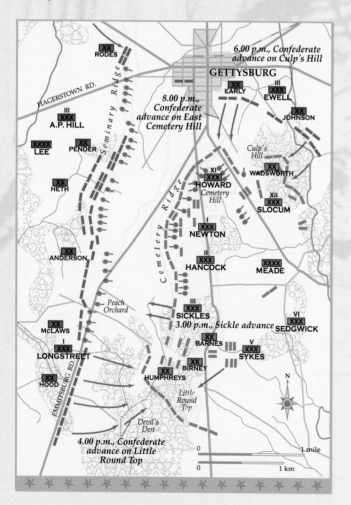

Map labels:
RODES, GETTYSBURG, EARLY, EWELL, JOHNSON, A.P. HILL, LEE, PENDER, HETH, ANDERSON, McLAWS, LONGSTREET, HOOD, HUMPHREYS, BIRNEY, SICKLES, BARNES, SYKES, HANCOCK, NEWTON, SLOCUM, WADSWORTH, HOWARD, MEADE, SEDGWICK, SYKES

6.00 p.m., Confederate advance on Culp's Hill

8.00 p.m., Confederate advance on East Cemetery Hill

3.00 p.m., Sickle advance

4.00 p.m., Confederate advance on Little Round Top

HAGERSTOWN RD.
EMMITSBURG RD.
Seminary Ridge
Cemetery Ridge
Culp's Hill
Cemetery Hill
Peach Orchard
Little Round Top
Devil's Den

0 ... 1 mile
0 ... 1 km

BACKGROUND Maj. Gen. John F. Reynolds, leading three corps of the Army of the Potomac in the opening phase at Gettysburg, is shot and mortally wounded while bringing forces forward to McPherson's Woods.

Lee arrived with a fresh division of Hill's corps, as more of Ewell's men came down the Harrisburg Road commanded by Lieutenant General Jubal Early. The XI Corps was overwhelmed and retreated through Gettysburg. Savage fighting in McPherson's Woods, meanwhile, drove the I Corps back. In the late afternoon Lee rode forward and observed the withdrawing Federal forces. Although Longstreet reminded his superior that defensive tactics were the watchword for the campaign, Lee was ready for a fight and indicated he wished to attack the Federals on Cemetery Ridge.

The retreating Federals passed through Gettysburg to East Cemetery Hill, a rallying point designated by II Corps commander Major General Winfield Scott Hancock. Sent forward by Meade, Hancock concluded that Gettysburg was ideal for fighting a defensive battle. Artillery on East Cemetery Hill discouraged an advance by Ewell on the Federal right. It was the best opportunity the Rebels had for an advantage as Union forces continued to arrive throughout the night.

By sunrise on July 2, the two great armies were separated by a mile of fields, orchards, and woods. The second day's battle could have been decisive had the assaults planned by Lee resulted in the rout of the Army of the Potomac.

Lee proposed that Longstreet form an attack on the Union left, while Ewell moved on the Union right and attacked if possible. On the other side of the Emmitsburg Road, Meade, who had arrived during the night, was described by an aide as "quick, bold, cheerful and hopeful." The Federal line extended in a fish-hook pattern from Culp's Hill and Cemetery Hill in the north, to just short of Big and Little Round Top in the south. With the afternoon arrival of the last Federal units, Major General Sedgwick's VI Corps, and Stuart's cavalry, more than 170,000 men were assembled at Gettysburg. The decisive phase of the battle now began.

"Oh, you dead, who at Gettysburg have baptized with your blood the second birth of freedom in America, how you are to be envied. I rise from the grave whose wet clay I have passionately kissed, and I look up and I see Christ spanning the battlefield—his right hand opens the gates of paradise, and with his left, he beckons to those mutilated, bloody, swollen forms to ascend."

NEW YORK TIMES REPORTER
SAMUEL WILKESON, WHO LOST A SON
ON THE FIRST DAY'S BATTLE,
JULY 1, 1863, GETTYSBURG

GETTYSBURG—THE HIGH WATER MARK OF THE CONFEDERACY

ON HIS OWN INITIATIVE, at about 3.00 p.m., Major General Daniel E. Sickles advanced his III Corps beyond the Federal line to the Peach Orchard. About this time, Lieutenant General James Longstreet launched his much-delayed offensive. Major General John Bell Hood led a staggered attack just south of the Peach Orchard aimed at Little Round Top. The hill had been left exposed by the Federals until Meade's chief engineer, Brigadier General Gouverneur Warren, discovered the error and rushed troops to the position. Fierce combat ensued until the Southerners were driven back. The Union left on Little Round Top, held by the 20th Maine, and the Union right, now held by the 140th New York, secured the southern end of the Federal line.

The battle continued to rage in the Peach Orchard, Devil's Den, Rose's Farm, and the Wheatfield, as Longstreet's corps became fully committed. In the Wheatfield, six Confederate attacks were driven back by six Federal counterattacks. A.P. Hill's corps failed to support the advance by Longstreet, a Confederate advance along Plum Run was turned back, and, except for sniper fire from Rebel positions in Devil's Den, the fighting in that sector ended for the day.

It was 6.00 p.m. before General Ewell began his demonstration. Confederates advanced against Culp's Hill, from where most of the Federal troops had been withdrawn. The

BELOW A portion of the huge cyclorama painting of the Battle of Gettysburg that captures the Pickett-Pettigrew charge on a 360-degree permanent mural. The work was unveiled in Chicago in 1883 after lead artist Paul Philippoteaux researched the scene by traveling to Gettysburg and consulting with former Union generals.

RIGHT The culmination of Lee's efforts at Gettysburg was a massive charge against the center on the afternoon of July 3—the Pickett-Pettigrew charge. Eleven brigades of Confederates marched across open fields and into the heart of the Federal line held by Brig. Gen. John Gibbon's division. Though some North Carolinians crested the ridge at the Angle, the assault was repulsed, and later Lee took full responsibility for its failure.

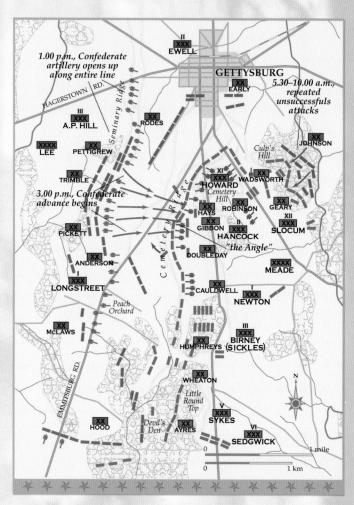

July 2 and 3, 1863

1.00 p.m., Confederate artillery opens up along entire line

5.30–10.00 a.m., repeated unsuccessfuls attacks

3.00 p.m., Confederate advance begins

"the Angle"

Peach Orchard

Devil's Den

Little Round Top

Confederates were prevented from taking it by the brigade of George Sears Greene, and only managed a toehold on the lower summit. At 8.00 p.m., North Carolinians and the Louisiana Tigers charged East Cemetery Hill, driving the XI Corps back on the Federal artillery. However, General Hancock rushed reinforcements to the hill and drove the Confederates back.

At a meeting with his senior generals that night, Meade indicated Lee would attack the center of the Federal line the next day. Over at the Thompson House, Lee's headquarters, Longstreet proposed a flanking movement by Big Round Top. But Lee instead announced a plan that would fulfill Meade's prediction.

In the predawn hours of July 3, fighting resumed on Culp's Hill, as Major General Henry Slocum's XII Corps fought an almost seven-hour battle to dislodge the Confederates. The

Federal right was secured and the battlefield entered a period of relative calm until 1.00 p.m.

Then, more than 150 Confederate cannons began the most formidable artillery bombardment ever staged by the South. The Union responded with a like number of guns, and the two-hour cannon duel was heard more than 150 miles away at Pittsburg.

Lee selected a division from his native Virginia, led by Major General George Pickett, to charge the Union center. On Pickett's left were North Carolinians under Brigadier General James J. Pettigrew. Eleven brigades in all advanced. At 3.00 p.m., the Confederate infantry began the nearly three-quarter-mile march over the open fields between the two ridges. Their objective was a copse of trees situated at approximately the middle of the Union line.

As the Confederates crossed the Emmitsburg Road, Federal artillery began to create gaps in their lines of battle. Major General John Gibbon rushed reinforcements to the area. Some Southerners made it over the stone wall in front of the Union artillery, but were quickly shot down or captured in the face of determined counterattack. The Confederates fell back, retreating across the Emmitsburg Road. Of the 12,500 men that went forward, two out of every three failed to return to the lines.

There was little action for the rest of July 3. Several miles to the east, General J.E.B. Stuart's cavalry was bested by Federal cavalry under Brigadier General David Gregg, while on the Union left another Federal cavalry advance failed to drive the Rebels from the base of Big Round Top. Southwest of Gettysburg, at Fairfield, Rebel horsemen overpowered the 6th U.S. Cavalry of Brigadier General Wesley Merritt.

On July 4, rains came to Gettysburg. Both sides anticipated renewed fighting, but none took place. That evening Lee and his battered army quietly retraced their steps from Virginia. With more than 20,000 casualties and thousands of prisoners now in his charge, Meade did not pursue.

On November 18, 1863, President Abraham Lincoln took a train from Washington to Gettysburg. The next day, he attended the function for which he was invited at the last

ABOVE A Federal cannon is moved from its position on Cemetery Hill as two brigades of Confederates storm the hill at twilight on July 2. Maj. Gen. Hancock brought reinforcements to the area just as the Rebels were cresting the hill and overtaking the guns of the XI Corps.

BACKGROUND Culp's Hill was the scene of savage fighting as veterans from Maj. Gen. Edward Johnson's division attacked a single brigade of Federals holding the hill after most of the XII Corps was sent to aid the Federal left. The Rebels secured a toehold but the fighting continued throughout the night when the rest of the XII Corps soldiers returned to claim their breastworks.

minute to speak. The featured speaker was the statesman and orator Edward Everett, whose two-hour speech at the dedication of the National Soldiers' Cemetery on Cemetery Hill was well received by a large crowd. But the world will never forget Lincoln's two-minute address that followed. The Gettysburg Address is one of the masterpieces of the English language and expresses the importance and meaning both of the Battle of Gettysburg and the American Civil War.

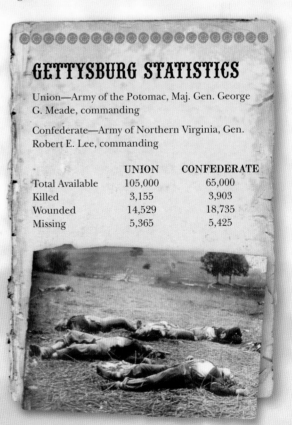

GETTYSBURG STATISTICS

Union—Army of the Potomac, Maj. Gen. George G. Meade, commanding

Confederate—Army of Northern Virginia, Gen. Robert E. Lee, commanding

	UNION	CONFEDERATE
Total Available	105,000	65,000
Killed	3,155	3,903
Wounded	14,529	18,735
Missing	5,365	5,425

THE COASTAL WAR

AT THE OUTSET of the Civil War it became apparent to Northern leaders that amphibious operations would be necessary along the 3,000-mile Southern coast, to capture ports, obtain coaling stations for ships on blockade duty, and to disrupt supplies to Confederate forces. Lacking vessels, Rebels relied on innovation and technology to defend their harbors. Their most successful tools were mines, called torpedoes by the South and "infernal machines" by Northern skippers, who risked significant damage if they encountered one of them.

The coastal war began with the seizure of Cape Hatteras, on North Carolina's Outer Banks, in August 1861. This toe-hold was extended in 1862 when Brigadier General Ambrose Burnside's forces captured Roanoke Island, Fort Macon, and New Bern, North Carolina's second-largest port.

Federal warships under Flag Officer Samuel Dupont took Port Royal, South Carolina on November 7, 1861. The Federal army then established bases at Hilton Head and Beaufort, South Carolina, to stage operations aimed at other Southeast Atlantic ports. The Confederacy sent Robert E. Lee to the area to counter the threat.

Charleston was bypassed by the Federals in favor of less fortified harbors such as Fernandina, Jacksonville, and St. Augustine, Florida. A more difficult challenge was Savannah, Georgia's most important port, guarded by Fort Pulaski.

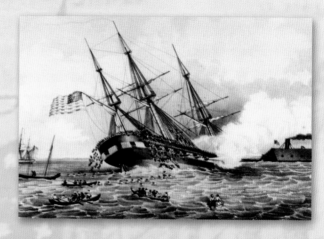

ABOVE C.S.S. *Virginia* maneuvers away from the sinking U.S.S. *Cumberland* after ramming the wooden vessel on March 8, 1862. Cannon shot fired from the ships of the Federal blockade squadron bounced off the *Virginia's* iron casemate.

BACKGROUND Federal soldiers under Brig. Gen. Ambrose E. Burnside storm the Confederate works south of New Bern, North Carolina, on March 14, 1862, capturing the strategic city later that day.

RIGHT The *H.L. Hunley,* seen here on a Charleston pier in a painting by soldier-artist Conrad Wise Chapman, was an ingenious, though dangerous, submarine. Powered by eight crewmen turning a crank, it was able to ram a torpedo into the stern of U.S.S. *Housatonic* on February 17, 1864, though the vessel and its crew were lost in the sinking ship's wake.

BELOW Sailors and officers of the U.S.S. *Monitor* relax on the steel deck of the ship. The large gun turret is seen in the background. Most Union ironclads were of a design similar to the *Monitor.* The Confederates built ironclads with large casemates similar to the *Virginia.*

Under the direction of engineering officer Captain Quincy A. Gillmore, the Federals placed large siege guns near the fort. On April 10, 1862, the bombardment of the fort began and Pulaski's garrison surrendered the next day.

Construction of gunboats was accelerated on both sides. The U.S. Navy officer in charge of Norfolk, Virginia, abandoned and burned the large naval facility there on April 20, 1861, but Confederate soldiers arrived at the Gosport Navy Yard in Portsmouth in time to save part of the burning frigate U.S.S. *Merrimack.* The Rebels began to rebuild her into an ironclad warship rechristened as C.S.S. *Virginia.* When a spy delivered plans for the *Virginia* to Washington, Secretary of the Navy Gideon Welles called for the building of an ironclad for the North in 100 days.

On March 8, 1862, the *Virginia,* with 10 guns and armor plating, steamed into Hampton Roads at the mouth of the James River. Shore batteries and guns on the blockade ships U.S.S. *Congress* and U.S.S. *Cumberland* opened fire. The *Virginia's* armor was impervious to the shelling within a few hours, the *Virginia* rammed and sank the *Cumberland* and crippled the *Congress.* Other Federal warships came upriver, but all ran aground. That night U.S.S. *Monitor,* the Union's just-completed ironclad, arrived in Hampton Roads and anchored near the grounded ship.

On the morning of March 9, the *Virginia* returned to Hampton Roads and encountered the "cheesebox on a raft," as some called the *Monitor,* guarding the *Minnesota.* Both vessels circled, searching for weaknesses. The battle raged for six hours until the commander of the *Monitor* was wounded and the ironclad steered for shallow water. The historic action was

DAVID GLASGOW FARRAGUT

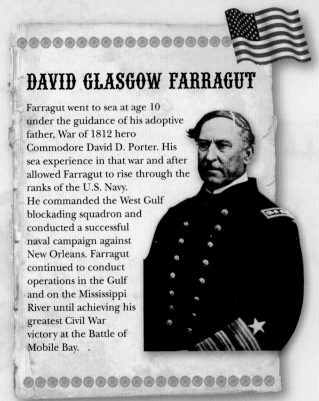

Farragut went to sea at age 10 under the guidance of his adoptive father, War of 1812 hero Commodore David D. Porter. His sea experience in that war and after allowed Farragut to rise through the ranks of the U.S. Navy. He commanded the West Gulf blockading squadron and conducted a successful naval campaign against New Orleans. Farragut continued to conduct operations in the Gulf and on the Mississippi River until achieving his greatest Civil War victory at the Battle of Mobile Bay. .

"Damn the torpedoes, four bells. Captain Drayton, go ahead. Do it, full speed."

ADMIRAL FARRAGUT DIRECTING THE CAPTAIN OF HIS FLAGSHIP TO RUN THE FORTS AND BATTERIES OF MOBILE BAY, AUGUST 5, 1864

Du Pont was replaced by Rear Admiral John A. Dahlgren, who worked with Brigadier General Quincy Gillmore, the army's siege expert. Gillmore planned to use siege guns to exploit a weakness in the side of Fort Sumter facing Morris Island. The Federals advanced on Morris Island in the summer of 1863, but were stopped at Battery Wagner. The siege continued and Fort Sumter was reduced to rubble. None of these Federal operations succeeded in eliminating the stubborn Rebel resistance in Charleston, and the city held out until 1865. The Confederates also terrorized Federal ships with torpedoes and a short-lived submarine, *H.L. Hunley.*

In August 1864, Rear Admiral David G. Farragut began the long-awaited investment of Mobile by running his warships and ironclads past Forts Morgan and Gaines, which guarded the entrance to Mobile Bay. He destroyed several Confederate ships in the process and forced the forts to surrender, but Mobile did not capitulate until near the end of the war.

considered a draw, but the *Monitor* prevented the destruction of the Federal fleet at Hampton Roads. The two ships never faced each other again. The *Virginia* was destroyed by the Rebels as the Union army threatened the tidewater area and the *Monitor* sank in the Atlantic while being towed to Charleston in December 1862.

In early 1863, the Federal blockade of Southern ports left only four trading centers remaining to the Confederates. These were Galveston, Texas, Mobile, Alabama; Wilmington, North Carolina, guarded by powerful forts; and Charleston, South Carolina, the cradle of the Confederacy.

Encouraged by the performance of U.S.S. *Monitor*, Welles accelerated the building of more Monitor class ironclads. Rear Admiral Samuel du Pont's nine-ship flotilla attempted to enter Charleston Harbor on April 7, 1863. However, tremendous crossfire in the channel between Fort Sumter and Fort Moultrie forced him to turn back.

ABOVE The brand-new ironclad U.S.S. *Monitor* challenges the South's C.S.S. *Virginia* in the first battle of iron ships, March 9, 1862 at Hampton Roads, Virginia.

LEFT On August 5, 1864, Rear Admiral David G. Farragut ran his warships past two forts at the mouth of Mobile Bay, but his lead ironclad hit a torpedo (mine) and his column plunged into confusion. Braving the torpedoes, Farragut kept the line of ships moving past the forts and the Confederate squadron, which included the powerful ironclad C.S.S. *Tennessee.*

THE VICKSBURG CAMPAIGN

A NUMBER OF ATTEMPTS TO CAPTURE Vicksburg before summer 1863 had failed. Then, in May and June, Major General Ulysses S. Grant placed the city under siege through a brilliant campaign, running gunboats and other naval craft past the city at night and following up with a sweeping flanking march of his army to the land side of the city.

By early June 1862, Federal naval forces under the command of Flag Officer David G. Farragut and others had completed the capture or control of the Mississippi River except Port Hudson, Louisiana, and Vicksburg, Mississippi. Even though Farragut's ships later engaged the batteries at both locations, neither of these impregnable bastions would fall without army support.

By late fall of 1862, the job of capturing Vicksburg fell to the commander in whom Lincoln had the greatest confidence: Ulysses S. Grant. "I like this man, he fights," Lincoln remarked. Grant's first problem was getting his troops to Vicksburg. Various attempts were made to move the force from its base in Northeast Mississippi toward Vicksburg, but these were thwarted, mostly by raids on Union supplies and communication by Rebel cavalry units. Finally, Grant, determined to approach Vicksburg from the west or south,

December 1862– July 1863

ABOVE This photograph shows the Shirley House, also known as the White House, at Vicksburg from behind the Federal front lines. Beyond the Shirley House were the Rebel defenses. Union sappers and miners dug approaches ever closer to the Confederate lines and took cover in these shelters (foreground) when coming under artillery fire or during breaks.

LEFT Maj. Gen. Ulysses S. Grant scored a major victory at Vicksburg, but it came at a cost. At Vicksburg and beyond, his strategic use of the means of war would be necessary to defeat a determined foe.

relocated his army group to Northeast Louisiana. Yet, troop transports and gunboats still had to pass Vicksburg's high bluffs and well-placed artillery. Several unique approaches were tried, including continuing the work started by Farragut on a canal to divert the Mississippi River away from Vicksburg's guns. Finally, Rear Admiral David D. Porter ran the Vicksburg batteries on the night of April 16, 1863, a move timed to coincide with a lavish Confederate ball being held in the city. The run of gunboats and transports was successful, and they were met by infantry units that had marched down the Louisiana bank.

The Federals then tested a crossing at Grand Gulf, where Confederate batteries were commanded by the very capable Brigadier General John S. Bowen. On April 29, Porter's gunboats dueled with Grand Gulf's two forts, Wade and Cobun. After five and a half hours Porter broke off the engagement, and the navy commander convinced Grant that Grand Gulf's defenses were too strong. Finally, on April 30, Grant's first units landed near Port Gibson, south of Grand Gulf, and a long, circuitous march to Vicksburg began, accompanied by a string of Federal victories at Port Gibson, Raymond, Jackson, Champion Farm, and the Big Black River.

The Vicksburg garrison, under the command of Lieutenant General John C. Pemberton, retreated

VICKSBURG STATISTICS

Vicksburg Assaults and Siege

Union—Army of the Tennessee, Maj. Gen. Ulysses
S. Grant, commanding

Confederate—Vicksburg Garrison, Lt. Gen. John
C. Pemberton, commanding

	UNION	CONFEDERATE
Total Engaged	70,000	30,000
Killed and Wounded	4,373	958
(incl. U.S. Navy)		
Surrendered		9,042
and Paroled		

Gen. Joseph E. Johnston had approximately
30,000 soldiers outside Vicksburg who were not
engaged in the siege.

to the safety of the town's defenses, closely pursued by
Grant's force. After two largely unsuccessful attacks on the
fortress on May 19 and 22, the Federals began siege
operations. As the weeks passed, the besieged Rebels hoped
for relief from a force being assembled outside Vicksburg by
General Joseph E. Johnston. But Johnston was unwilling to
challenge Grant's large and well-organized force, a position
that drew heavy criticism of the general. As one Alabama
newspaper quipped, Johnston was "fighting Grant daily by
giving him a terrible letting-alone."

With hope for a rescue failing, Pemberton initiated
surrender overtures, timed to coincide with Independence
Day, which Pemberton, as a Northerner, believed would allow
for more liberal terms from the patriotic Federals. After some
negotiations, terms were worked out that surrendered the
city and on July 4, 1863, the Confederate defenders marched
out of Vicksburg and stacked their arms.

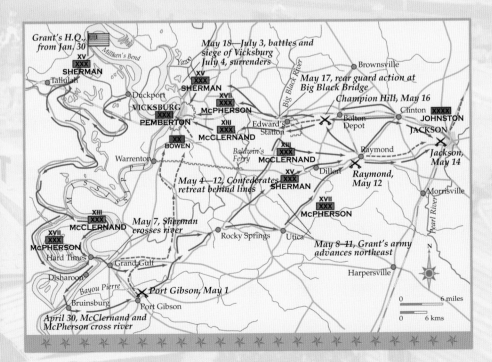

ABOVE Rear Admiral David D. Porter's gunboats
take the lead in a run of Federal vessels past the
Vicksburg batteries on the night of April 16, 1863.
A slow response by the Confederates allowed the
flotilla to pass with little damage.

LEFT U.S. Grant's forces landed below Vicksburg
on April 30 and began a series of successful
marches and battles to drive the Confederates
into their prepared defense line outside
Vicksburg. Federal assaults on those defenses
began on May 19, centering at Stockade Redan.
Only a small foothold was gained and another
assault was launched on May 22 across a broad
front. Once again valiant effort saved the Rebel
works and the Federals began siege operations
at Vicksburg.

BACKGROUND The wharves of Vicksburg. Before
the war, they were among the busiest on the
Mississippi, carrying passengers and cargo up and
down the river.

DESPITE WASHINGTON'S impatience for action, Major General William S. Rosencrans's Army of the Cumberland remained in its camps after its defeat of the Confederates at Stones River in January 1863. It was mid-June before Rosecrans left Murfreesboro, but when he did move, it was with speed and precision.

Rosecrans maneuvered his force through three mountain gaps, ending up on both flanks of his opponent, General Braxton Bragg, who fell back to Chattanooga to protect his supply line. Washington immediately prodded Rosecrans to attack Bragg and drive the Rebels from East Tennessee, but the Federal general hoped to outmaneuver Bragg and force a Confederate withdrawal without a major battle. He advanced part of his force over the mountains west of Chattanooga while sending one corps to feign a crossing of the Tennessee River. The ruse was effective. On September 7, Bragg evacuated Chattanooga without a fight to protect his railroad supply line from Atlanta.

BELOW In the two-day battle of Chickamauga, the nearly parallel north-south lines of Federal and Confederate forces held against assaults from their foe. Then on September 20, James Longstreet launched an attack on the Federal center, unaware that a mistake had caused a gap in the Federal line at his point of attack. Rebel veterans rushed through, driving William S. Rosecrans and much of his force from the field. But George Thomas repositioned his line on Snodgrass Hill and held off repeated assaults until his soldiers could make an orderly withdrawal.

September–November 186

AMBROSE E. BURNSIDE

Ambrose Everett Burnside was one of the most energetic, if not successful, commanders of the Civil War. Born in Indiana, he attended West Point, served on the Western frontier, and resigned to begin manufacturing a quality carbine that bore his name. He lost the business, but others benefited from his patents. His wartime record was uneven— Lincoln praised him for leadership at First Manassas, in coastal North Carolina, and at Knoxville. Hesitancy and poor judgment marred his record at Antietam, Fredericksburg, and Petersburg. .

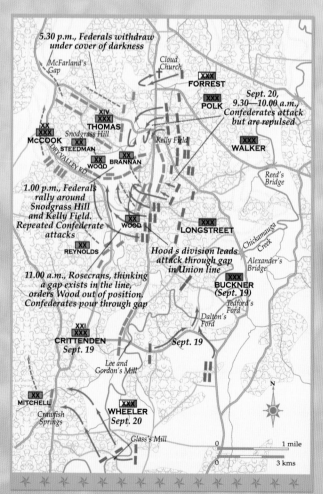

Rosecrans's late summer campaign drew in reinforcements on both sides. Robert E. Lee sent Lieutenant General James Longstreet and most of his corps from Virginia on a 900-mile rail trip through the Carolinas and Atlanta to aid Bragg.

Rosecrans continued the advance. Reports from deserters and civilians strengthened his belief that Bragg's army was in full retreat. In fact, Bragg was playing his own game of deception, looking for a chance to attack part of Rosecrans's force, spread out on a 40-mile front. Rosecrans recognized that his army was too scattered, and began to concentrate his army on Major General Thomas Crittenden's position at Lee and Gordon's Mill. By September 18, his army formed a continuous line behind a rambling creek with the Cherokee name of Chickamauga (the river of death).

Bragg hoped to turn the Federal left flank, but the sluggishness of his corps commanders delayed the attack. On September 19, Bragg discovered that Rosecrans had tightened his line during the night. Both sides fought stubbornly and the Army of the Cumberland held its ground. Bragg planned another attack for the next morning. Longstreet, who had just

ABOVE Maj. Gen. George Thomas, USA, was a pre-war U.S. Army veteran officer from Virginia who alienated family and friends by remaining loyal to the Union. He had a consistent record of success in commanding forces in Kentucky, Tennessee, and Georgia but his loyalty was incorrectly doubted by many in power until late in the war.

arrived on the field with two brigades, was given command of the Confederate left wing, Lieutenant General Leonidas Polk the right. During the fighting on September 20, Federal soldiers hidden in a tree line caused Rosecrans to shift forces. When Longstreet launched an attack on the Union center he was unaware of the gap, but his aggressive veterans were able to exploit it to great advantage.

Crittenden and Major General Alexander McCook fled the field with their broken ranks, together with Rosecrans and his staff, as Longstreet pushed brigade after brigade into the vacuum created by the retreating Federals. Unshaken by this turn of events, Major General George Thomas, with reinforcements sent from Rossville Gap by Major General Gordon Granger, held the Union left, making a stand on Snodgrass Hill. He then conducted an orderly withdrawal after dark to meet the rest of the Army of the Cumberland, which had fled the field earlier.

This bloody battle, with the greatest casualties of the Western theater, bolstered Southern spirits. Yet Bragg was appalled by his own 20,000 killed, wounded, and missing at Chickamauga, and his pursuit of the Federals was painfully slow. The Rebels advanced to Lookout Mountain and Missionary Ridge, virtually surrounding Rosecrans's army in Chattanooga.

Alarmed by the situation in Tennessee, Lincoln appointed Major General Ulysses S. Grant to overall command in the region, and Grant headed to Chattanooga. Two corps from the Army of the Potomac under Major General Joseph Hooker were ordered to join him there. George Thomas, the "Rock of Chickamauga," replaced Rosecrans in command of the Army of the Cumberland. With the arrival of Major General William Sherman's force, the total Federal force in Chattanooga amounted to 70,000. Grant positioned his troops in Chattanooga to stage a breakout. He sent Sherman to the north to attack the right flank of Bragg's line on Missionary Ridge. To the southwest, Hooker was to seize Lookout Mountain and then approach Missionary Ridge from the south.

STORMING AND CAPTURE OF LOOKOUT MOUNTAIN.

By Major General JOSEPH HOOKER, Commanding.

The attack began on November 24.

Hooker's men drove the Rebels from key positions on Lookout Mountain while Sherman gained a foothold on a northern extension of Missionary Ridge. Thomas's force was kept near the city to guard the center of the line. The next day, with Lookout Mountain in Federal hands, but Sherman's southward drive stalled on Missionary Ridge, Grant asked Thomas to demonstrate against the Rebel center. At 4.00 p.m., the Army of the Cumberland troops advanced against the Confederates at the base of Missionary Ridge. Regiment after regiment raced to the top shouting "Chickamauga! Chickamauga!" The Rebels fell back in a rout.

Sherman and Hooker linked their forces with Thomas's that night and they then pushed the Confederate force into Georgia. Bragg soon resigned his command.

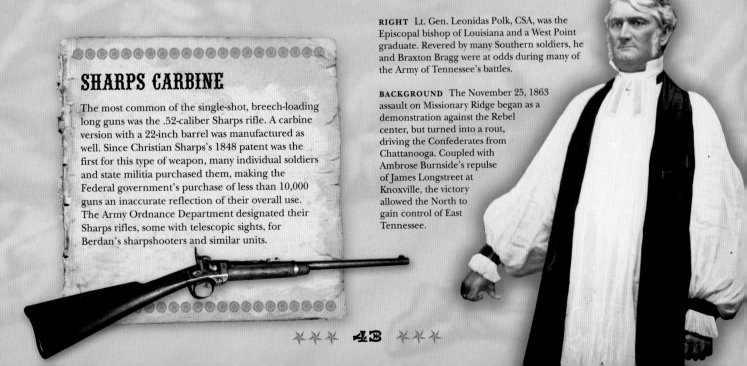

SHARPS CARBINE

The most common of the single-shot, breech-loading long guns was the .52-caliber Sharps rifle. A carbine version with a 22-inch barrel was manufactured as well. Since Christian Sharps's 1848 patent was the first for this type of weapon, many individual soldiers and state militia purchased them, making the Federal government's purchase of less than 10,000 guns an inaccurate reflection of their overall use. The Army Ordnance Department designated their Sharps rifles, some with telescopic sights, for Berdan's sharpshooters and similar units.

WAR ON THE HIGH SEAS

MOST OF THE CIVIL WAR operations of the tradition-rich U.S. Navy, and the Confederacy's fledgling navy, occurred on the nation's rivers and in coastal areas. However, both sides used ocean-going craft, and hundreds of salt-water seamen and officers sought military and political advantage for their respective causes.

At the beginning of the war, the Federal navy was undermanned and a number of key officers joined the Confederate navy. Many ships were stationed abroad while a few were captured in Southern ports. This weakened force was charged with enforcing the blockade of the South, which began slowly. Many "blockade-runners," ships carrying cotton abroad and returning with war and luxury goods, made their runs to Southern ports without incident. Gradually, the size and power of the Federal fleet improved the effectiveness of the blockade and in 1862, one out of every seven runners was captured.

The Confederates believed that, with England and France dependent on Southern cotton, the British Navy would come to the Rebels' aid, thus compensating for the South's weak sea-going navy. This never happened, but an incident in 1861 did have the potential to turn Great Britain into an enemy of the North. In November, Captain Charles Wilkes, commander of U.S.S. *San Jacinto*, stopped the British mail-steamer *Trent* in the Caribbean, and removed two Confederate envoys to Europe, James Mason and John Slidell. The incident created a tense situation between Washington and London, until Secretary of State William Seward arranged a diplomatic

BELOW The Federal warship *Pensacola* in a festive display of naval tradition with crewmen standing on the yardarms.

solution that saw the Southern officials released. Great Britain and France remained neutral throughout the Civil War, but both countries tacitly permitted Confederate agent James Bulloch to make arrangements for the construction and purchase of warships for the Rebels.

This was important as the South lacked any shipbuilding facilities of its own. Bulloch sought specially designed ships to seek out and destroy the Union merchant marine. Commerce raiding was the traditional means for an inferior naval power to damage its enemy, and even before Bulloch delivered a single ship to the South, the most successful Confederate captain had already gone to work. Former U.S. Navy commander Raphael Semmes converted a steamer into the cruiser C.S.S. *Sumter* and captured 17 U.S. merchant vessels before his ship was retired. In August 1862, Semmes assumed command of the most famous Confederate raider, C.S.S. *Alabama*, a vessel Bulloch had had built privately in Liverpool. Within 18 months, Semmes and the *Alabama* had captured 64 Federal merchantmen and destroyed U.S.S. *Hatteras* off the Texas coast.

Other commerce raiders flourished, particularly in the early years of the war. Some ships taken as prizes by the Rebels were turned into raiders or became blockade-runners. C.S.S. *Florida*, another Liverpool-built raider, took 24 prizes in 1862 under Captain James Maffitt. C.S.S. *Shenandoah* concentrated its efforts on the Northern whaling fleet in the Pacific.

By 1863, because of the damage caused by Semmes, Maffitt, and others, insurance rates for U.S. merchantmen skyrocketed. Many ships were re-registered under neutral flags, and shipping companies applied pressure on the Lincoln administration to go after the Confederate cruisers wherever they might lie, including international ports.

RAPHAEL SEMMES

Semmes, a veteran U.S. Navy commander, joined the Confederate States Navy when Alabama seceded. Semmes, who was also a lawyer and author, initiated the idea of Rebel commerce-raiding and was its most successful practitioner. After the loss of C.S.S. *Alabama*, Semmes returned to the South, was made Rear Admiral, and helped in the final defense of Richmond. Branded a pirate by the North, he was arrested. All charges were dropped and he eventually returned to Mobile to practice law and write.

ABOVE C.S.S. *Alabama* and U.S.S. *Kearsarge* do battle off the coast of France on June 19, 1864. The crew of the *Kearsarge* hung anchor chains over the sides of the ship, decreasing the effectiveness of the *Alabama's* shots.

In June 1864, the *Alabama* was in harbor at Cherbourg, France, and its presence was reported to Captain John Winslow, commander of U.S.S. *Kearsarge*, who determined to prevent the *Alabama's* escape. Cavalier and confident that the two wooden ships were evenly matched, Semmes challenged the *Kearsarge* to a one-on-one battle, and Winslow was happy to oblige.

On the morning of June 19, about six miles off the French coast, the two ships engaged in the most famous high seas duel of the Civil War. After an hour of gallant fighting, the *Alabama* was finished. Semmes and most of his crew were rescued by a British passenger vessel, which was observing the action.

The legacy of Rebel commerce-raiding remained long past the end of the Confederacy. The U.S. merchant fleet, worn down by destruction and the transfer of ships' registries to neutral powers, would never regain the dominant position that it enjoyed in the middle of the 19th century. And the blockade, which all but ended with the capture of Fort Fisher in January 1865 and the resulting closure of the South's last port at Wilmington, North Carolina, was one of the major contributors to Northern victory in the Civil War.

ABOVE On January 15, 1865, Brig. Gen. Alfred H. Terry led a combined force of Federal soldiers, sailors, and marines, supported by naval guns, against imposing Fort Fisher at the mouth of the Cape Fear River. The victory closed the South's last major port, Wilmington, North Carolina.

BACKGROUND Musicians pose on the deck of a Union ship. Music played an important part in maintaining morale for Civil War sailors at sea, just as it did for soldiers in the field.

FOR THE FOURTH TIME in as many years, the Federals attempted to dislodge the Confederates from Virginia's Piedmont region and move on Richmond, against a Rebel force composed of General Robert E. Lee's Army of Northern Virginia. But in May of 1864, that Federal force was commanded by Lieutenant General Ulysses S. Grant.

Although Major General George G. Meade retained command of the Army of the Potomac, Grant decided how the army was to be used. Meade offered to resign, but Grant encouraged the hero of Gettysburg to stay in command and the two worked well together. Grant brought Major General Philip H. Sheridan east to head the Federal cavalry corps, while the infantry was led by Winfield Scott Hancock, Gouverneur Warren, Ambrose Burnside, and John Sedgewick.

Grant wanted to traverse the Wilderness as quickly as possible, but Lee would not allow the dense scrub forest to be crossed without a fight. On the morning of May 5, Confederate attacks began, and the Federals could not repulse Lee's troops, shielded as they were by the tangled forest. That night Lee anticipated the arrival of Lieutenant General Longstreet's corps from Gordonsville to back up Lieutenant General A.P. Hill's weakened corps on the right. The Federals did not wait for that to happen. In Grant's dawn attack on May 6, Hancock broke through and Lee, sensing disaster, personally rallied units on the Tapp Farm.

Longstreet arrived in time to launch a thunderous counterattack from two directions simultaneously. As the Federals fell back, Longstreet was caught in a crossfire and was seriously wounded by friendly fire. The Rebel advance stalled. On the other side of the Wilderness, Brigadier General John B. Gordon attacked the exposed northern flank of the Union line, capturing 600 Federals. Darkness halted this advance and Sedgwick stabilized the Union right. Grant's order on the morning of May 7 called not for a retreat, as in the previous

May–June 1864

PHILIP H. SHERIDAN

Philip Henry Sheridan, the son of Irish immigrants, had a temper that caused him to clash frequently with others. On finally receiving combat command, he turned his pugnacious qualities on the enemy. His soldiers fought aggressively at Perryville, Stones River, Chickamauga, and Missionary Ridge. He quickly gained rank and Grant's attention. In 1864, as Grant's cavalry chief, he raided and fought Rebel horsemen with equal skill. His successes in the Shenandoah Valley made him a key commander in the ultimate victory.

Virginia campaigns, but a march to Spotsylvania Court House, skirting Lee's right flank.

Sheridan's cavalry struck out on their own to screen the march to Spotsylvania from Major General J.E.B. Stuart's Rebel horsemen. Sheridan's troopers skirmished and scored a major victory at Yellow Tavern on May 11, in which the fearless Stuart was mortally wounded. Major General R.H. Anderson, commanding the I Corps in place of the wounded Longstreet, moved to a strategic position west of Spotsylvania Court House. The rapidly marching Federals did the same.

Attacks by the V Corps were repulsed by Anderson's Confederates, who were protected by hastily constructed breastworks, which they expanded into an elaborate system of earthworks. On May 9, Grant sent Hancock's corps to

LEFT The Battle of Spotsylvania, May 8–20, 1864. The shift of the Army of the Potomac around Gen. Robert E. Lee's right flank was immediately challenged at the key Spotsylvania Court House crossroads. Both sides quickly entrenched. Hancock failed to turn Lee's left on May 9 but a thrust at the Confederate center the next evening by Col. Emory Upton spawned a general assault early on the 12th by the entire II Corps. Although the Rebel line was broken, a new one was established and a stalemate continued until Grant ordered a flanking march on May 21.

Map

N
0 ___ 1/2 mile
0 ___ 1/2 km

BROCK RD.

VI | XXX | WRIGHT
II | XXX | HANCOCK
XXXX | GRANT (MEADE)
XXX | EWELL

May 19 (Confederate "forced reconnaissance" turned back at Harris Farm)

May 12

"Bloody Angle" (Federal attack repulsed by Confederate counterattack, May 12)

VI | XXX | SEDGWICK | *May 10*

"Mule Shoe Salient" (abandoned May 13 to new line)

V | XXX | WARREN | *May 10*

May 10

XX | KERSHAW
XXX | EWELL
IX | XXX | BURNSIDE
V | XXX | WARREN

May 12

II | XXX | HANCOCK

May 9

Laurel Hill

XX | FIELD
XXX | R.H. ANDERSON
XX | HETH
XXX | EARLY

May 14 (Federals concentrate on Fredricksburg Rd., abandoning trenches on May 20)

Block House Bridge

May 10

XXXX | LEE

Po River

SHADY GROVE CHURCH RD.

SPOTSYLVANIA COUNTY

Spotsylvania Court House

May 21

XXX | A.P. HILL

IX | XXX | BURNSIDE

FREDRICKSBURG RD.

turn the Confederate left, but rough terrain slowed the advance enough for Lee to shift his troops. The following evening, the Federals attacked the center of the Confederate line, an imposing set of fortifications called the Mule Shoe. Twelve regiments assaulted the breastworks, but the attack failed to breach the ramparts.

Grant ordered a new assault on the Mule Shoe in the pre-dawn hours of May 12 with Hancock's entire corps. Once again the determined Southerners successfully resisted the attack. After 21 hours of fighting, Lee established a new defensive line. Despite five more days of skirmishing, the Rebel line at Spotsylvania Court House held.

Grant learned of Major General Franz Sigel's defeat in the Shenandoah Valley at New Market on May 15. This prompted Grant to order another turning of the Confederate right flank. On May 20, the Army of the Potomac broke camp and headed southeast to the North Anna River. The river, the last strong defensive line north of Richmond, was immediately challenged by Grant, but Lee quickly established a defensive position that held.

Grant also had to contend with the failings of another politically appointed general. Major General Benjamin Butler landed his Army of the James at Bermuda Hundred east of Richmond and entrenched, rather than strike a swift blow against General P.G.T. Beauregard's weak force. Reinforced, on May 16, Beauregard attacked the Federals near Drewry's Bluff, forcing Butler back to his entrenchments.

Grant sent Sheridan's cavalry on May 31 to take the crossroads at Cold Harbor. Meade ordered an attack on June 1, but Anderson's counterattack stabilized the situation. Grant decided to renew the attack but logistical problems postponed this until the morning of June 3. Lee strengthened his fragile lines. In 60 minutes just after dawn on June 3, the needless slaughter of 7,000 Federal troops occurred at the Battle of Cold Harbor. Grant took full responsibility.

Moving southeastward again, Grant confused Lee with a feint towards Glendale. He was able to slip around Lee's army, and drive toward the vital railroad city of Petersburg. On June 15, the lead Federal force, under Major General William F. Smith, failed to attack immediately; Hancock arrived at dawn to relieve Smith, but problems delayed the Union advance and Beauregard brought reinforcements from Drewry's Bluff.

Grant ordered assaults on the 17th and 18th, resulting in the Federals occupying the original works, but Beauregard ordered a new line constructed nearer to Petersburg. With Lee's veterans arriving, the Federals advanced on this line as well, but could not breach it. By nightfall the Union army had to settle into its own entrenchments. Beauregard and the still proud Army of Northern Virginia had given Lee what he needed to save Richmond and force the Federals into a protracted siege.

JUBAL EARLY

Jubal Early, an 1837 West Point graduate, served in Florida and then practiced law in Lynchburg, Virginia. Although he voted against secession in a state convention, Early became a staunch Confederate, bearing animosity against the North long after the War concluded. He was poor in reconnaissance but gained Lee's trust as a fighter. His independent raid to Washington in 1864 brought his greatest victory in the Battle of Monocacy, Maryland, but also saw his inglorious Shenandoah Valley defeat by Philip Sheridan.

SHERMAN'S CAMPAIGN FOR ATLANTA

IN THE OTHER major Federal campaign in the spring of 1864, Major General William T. Sherman and his army group applied the same flanking strategy as Lieutenant General Grant as they advanced down the line of the Western & Atlantic Railroad toward Atlanta. Opposing Sherman was the Army of Tennessee under General Joseph E. Johnston. Initially outnumbered two-to-one, Johnston received reinforcements from the Gulf Coast after Nathaniel Banks's failed Red River campaign.

With his force divided into three armies, the Army of the Cumberland, under Major General George Thomas, the Army of the Tennessee commanded by Major General James B. McPherson, and the Army of the Ohio led by Major General John Schofield, Sherman advanced on May 7.

On May 8, Sherman ordered two armies to test Confederate positions near Rocky Face Ridge. He pinned his hopes on a flanking move to Resaca by McPherson, who arrived east of there the same evening. But McPherson's advance on May 9 was contested by arriving Rebel reinforcements. Failure to make an all-out attack gave Johnston time to assemble his entire force at Resaca.

In two days of intense fighting, the Confederates held their positions until a division of the Army of the Tennessee established a bridgehead on the east bank of the Oostanaula

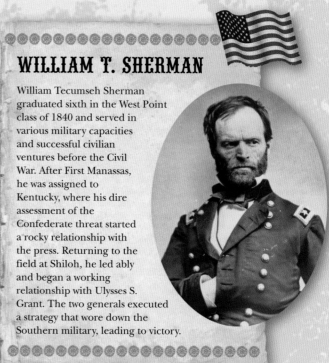

WILLIAM T. SHERMAN

William Tecumseh Sherman graduated sixth in the West Point class of 1840 and served in various military capacities and successful civilian ventures before the Civil War. After First Manassas, he was assigned to Kentucky, where his dire assessment of the Confederate threat started a rocky relationship with the press. Returning to the field at Shiloh, he led ably and began a working relationship with Ulysses S. Grant. The two generals executed a strategy that wore down the Southern military, leading to victory.

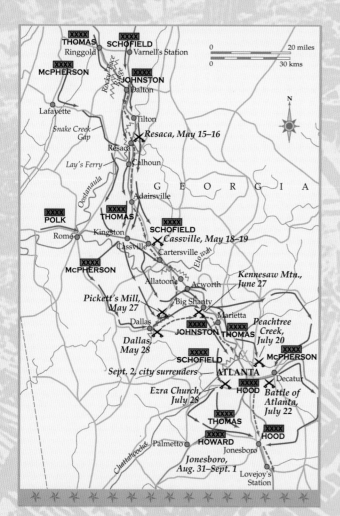

River, flanking Johnston and forcing him to withdraw. Sherman pursued, maneuvering to flank the Rebels at Adairsville, then skirmished briefly at Cassville, before Johnston withdrew across the Etowah River and into the Allatoona Mountains.

Johnston began to come under fire for his retreats, suffering harsh criticism from a commander with a battle-scarred body but a strong fighting spirit, Lieutenant General John Bell Hood. Yet Johnston's defensive tactics succeeded in protecting his smaller army. Sherman decided to shift his priority from destroying the Army of Tennessee to capturing the important manufacturing and rail city of Atlanta.

Packing 20 days' rations, Sherman sent his three armies southwest toward Dallas. Johnston again moved to block his advance. In battles at New Hope Church and Pickett's Mill on May 26 and 27, Federal advances were turned back. The Army of the Tennessee resisted a Rebel attack at Dallas on the 28th, as the Northerners dug their own formidable line of trenches.

LEFT The Campaign for Atlanta was fought in a series of battles and flanking moves in the mountains of northwest Georgia. When Maj. Gen. William T. Sherman's army group was stopped by Confederates of the Army of Tennessee under Gen. Joseph E. Johnston, Sherman's force would seek a way around the prepared positions by flanking the Rebels. This drove Johnston to fall back until Sherman crossed the Chattahoochee River and approached Atlanta's outer defenses.

Sherman's cavalry had secured Allatoona Pass by the time the armies moved to Dallas. As a result, he decided to move back to the rail line. However, torrential rains in early June turned the red clay Georgia roads into slippery quagmires. Johnston established a line on Brush, Pine, and Lost Mountains. It took two weeks for the Federals to follow, but when they arrived they pummeled the line with artillery fire. Lieutenant General Leonidas Polk was among the Confederates killed. Johnston now withdrew to a stronger line anchored on Big and Little Kennesaw Mountains. On June 22, he ordered Hood to protect the extreme left of the Confederate line. Hood then attacked Schofield's force at Kolb's Farm, suffering heavy casualties. Thinking Johnston had weakened the center of his line to protect his flanks, Sherman ordered a general assault at Kennesaw Mountain for June 27.

The bloody attack at Kennesaw was repulsed and Sherman had his fears of a direct assault on entrenchments manned by Confederate veterans confirmed. In a concurrent action, Schofield's soldiers advanced south of Kennesaw Mountain, where, finally, Sherman could see Atlanta before him.

Sherman once again put the bulk of his soldiers in front of Johnston's entrenchments to test them, while detaching smaller forces to find ways around the Rebels. Johnston was forced to fall back from Kennesaw Mountain to Smyrna, then to fortifications protecting the Chattahoochee River. Federal cavalry crossed and Johnston had to abandon the river line, falling back to Peachtree Creek on the night of July 9. Sherman, not wishing to test the strength of the imposing Confederate earthworks ringing the city, had his men begin to entrench outside the Rebel works to contain the enemy, while dispatching cavalry to destroy Atlanta's railroad link to the east.

Despite accomplishing much in rebuilding his army, Johnston's withdrawal tactics kept him at odds with the Confederate leadership. On July 18, John Bell Hood was appointed to replace him as commander of the Army of Tennessee.

RIGHT AND BACKGROUND These fortifications on the east side of Atlanta show the strength of the city's defenses. Built over the course of a year under orders from Georgia's governor, the 12-mile line encircled the city. Sherman respected the defenses and rather than assault them he chose to cut the railroads into Atlanta.

JOHNSTON'S REPLACEMENT as commander of the Army of Tennessee, the aggressive John Bell Hood, began a series of attacks to justify President Davis's confidence in him. On July 20, he attacked Thomas's army as it crossed Peachtree Creek. The Rebels took high casualties as their assault was turned back.

The fighting continued on the eastern approach to Atlanta on the 21st. That night, Hood ordered Major General William Hardee's corps on an all-night march to attack the exposed southern flank of McPherson's army. However, by the time the Rebel attack began on the afternoon of July 22, the Federals were in a position to defend against the maneuver. Though McPherson was mortally wounded early in the battle, Major General John "Blackjack" Logan rallied the Federal XV Corps and the Union line held. By day's end, Hood's second offensive had been turned back. Sherman then focused on destroying Atlanta's two remaining railroads.

On July 28, Hood launched a third attack on the Federal line's right flank at Ezra Church. The assault was repulsed, but Sherman's attempt to take the Atlanta & West Point Railroad was turned back. With only one rail line remaining open to Atlanta and a proud army within its fortifications, Sherman decided to lay siege to the city.

On August 30, John Bell Hood sent two corps under Hardee to intercept the Army of the Tennessee's march to Macon. A two-day battle at Jonesboro ending on September 1 resulted in a disastrous Rebel defeat, forcing Hood to abandon Atlanta. On September 3, Sherman wired Washington, "Atlanta is ours, and fairly taken."

The Confederate Army of Tennessee, however, was not destroyed. In late September, John Bell Hood, with the full support of President Davis, embarked on a mission to cut Sherman's lines of communications northwest to Tennessee. Sherman left an occupation force in Atlanta and started after Hood. After being repulsed at Allatoona Pass and other points along the railroad, Hood turned his army west and into the

JOHN BELL HOOD

Kentucky-born Hood is often remembered for his inspired leadership of the hard-fighting Texas Brigade. A poor student at West Point, Hood served in the pre-war Army, joined the Confederacy, and rose quickly through the officer ranks with a reputation as a ferocious fighter. Wounded at Gettysburg and Chickamauga, he lost his right leg and use of his left arm. Critical of General Joseph Johnston, Hood assumed command of the Army of Tennessee, then led it into a series of disastrous defeats.

mountains of north Alabama. Sherman gave up pursuit, returned to Atlanta, and wrote to Grant about his new idea—a march to Savannah, Georgia, continuing the war of destruction he had previously waged in places such as Meridian, Mississippi.

Grant and Lincoln recognized the logistical and psychological affects of cutting another line through the Deep South. Sherman departed Atlanta on November 15 with more than 60,000 troops divided into two columns, leaving Atlanta to demolition teams intent on destroying military, industrial, and government property.

Earlier, Sherman had dispatched George Thomas to Nashville, while John Schofield guarded south-central Tennessee from Rebel cavalry raids and a move by Hood. On November 21, Hood's Army of Tennessee, joined by Nathan B. Forrest's cavalry, left Florence, Alabama, on a march that Hood dreamed would carry them to the banks of the Ohio River and an eventual rendezvous with his former comrades in Virginia. But Hood allowed Schofield's smaller force to escape in front of him. Taking a defensive position at Franklin, Tennessee, Schofield drove off a desperate Confederate frontal assault

LEFT This dramatic lithograph shows Sherman's men at work tearing up track and destroying buildings of a railroad depot on the march to the sea. A family of ex-slaves, foreground, runs to the safety of the Federal soldiers. These refugees would prove to be a difficult and unexpected challenge to the forces in the campaign.

LEFT William T. Sherman stands at one of the Federal artillery batteries built for the siege of Atlanta. Photographer George Barnard followed Sherman's army group on the campaign and documented key moments and locations.

BACKGROUND The railroad depot at Allatoona Pass was a strategic location and fortified by two Federal forts, the Star Fort on the bluff at the left and the Eastern Redoubt on the right. Brig. Gen. John M. Corse successfully turned away a Rebel attack here on October 5, 1864 as John Bell Hood's army passed through northwest Georgia on the way to Tennessee.

on November 30. As Schofield escaped north, the Rebels mourned the loss of many in their ranks, including six generals killed in the battle.

Hood took his weakened force to Nashville. He expected reinforcements from the Trans-Mississippi region, but the Rebels would have to pass U.S. Navy patrols on the Mississippi. Thomas was in no hurry to move against Hood, a delay which worried Lincoln. As Grant prepared to travel to Tennessee to relieve him, Thomas launched a thunderous attack on December 15 and 16, crushing the Confederates with overwhelming numbers.

Many Rebels surrendered, others simply went home. Those remaining in Hood's army were pursued by Union cavalry and infantry until they reached Tupelo, Mississippi, in early January, where John Bell Hood resigned his command. Grant, who learned en route of the victory at Nashville, returned to City

Point and wired Thomas, "The armies operating against Richmond have fired 200 guns in honor of your great victory."

At virtually the same time as the Army of the Cumberland was driving the Rebels from Nashville, Sherman was arriving at Fort McAllister near Savannah. His southeastward march effectively destroyed the war-making capabilities of eastern Georgia, while his foraging parties allowed his swift columns to live off the land. There were problems to be dealt with— unauthorized looting by "bummers" and managing large groups of ex-slaves that followed the army—but these challenges did not diminish the effect of the march to the sea.

A Federal infantry assault on December 13 overwhelmed Fort McAllister, and caused the Confederate evacuation of Savannah on the night of December 20. Federal soldiers occupied the city unopposed. Before Sherman continued his march into South Carolina he paused to wire Lincoln: "I beg to present you as a Christmas gift the city of Savannah with 150 heavy guns and plenty of ammunition and also about 25,000 bales of cotton."

RIGHT The Battle of Atlanta, July 22, 1864, as portrayed in the Atlanta cyclorama painting. As Sherman attempted to capture the Georgia Railroad into the city on the east side, Hood launched a furious attack against the Army of the Tennessee in the area. Here, a hand-to-hand struggle is fought over the colors of the 15th Illinois.

PRISON CAMPS

WHEN MAJOR GENERAL William T. Sherman was attempting to break the siege of Atlanta in July 1864, he ordered a cavalry raid aimed at Macon, south of the city. The troopers under Major General George Stoneman had a special mission—to take the huge prisoner-of-war stockade at Andersonville. But Major General Joseph Wheeler's Confederate cavalry defeated Stoneman's force and captured part of it. The Federal general and his officers were themselves confined at Macon, while his enlisted troopers were imprisoned at Andersonville. Already notorious for its high death rate in the first six months of its operation, Andersonville, known officially to the Confederates as Camp Sumter, was built in the early part of 1864 to alleviate problems at overcrowded Richmond-area prisons, and to locate prisoners farther from the theaters of combat.

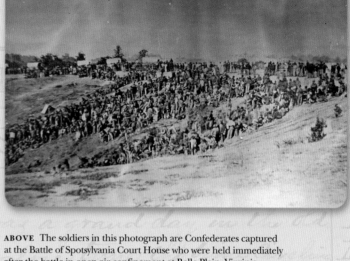

ABOVE The soldiers in this photograph are Confederates captured at the Battle of Spotsylvania Court House who were held immediately after the battle in open-air confinement at Belle Plain, Virginia.

Poor planning, a lack of supplies, and mismanagement quickly doomed the prison. The death rate was nearly 30 percent, the highest of all Civil War prisons. There were too many prisoners for the size of the stockade, a lack of shelter, food, and medical supplies, and a location that made good sanitation all but impossible. Prisoners fell into a state of despair, crossing the "dead line" to end their miserable existence, or preying on weaker prisoners.

The camp commandant, a Swiss-born self-proclaimed plantation doctor named Captain Heinrich Hartmann "Henry" Wirz, became a figure of hate, as stories of the atrocious conditions surfaced. Wirz did make some positive contributions, such as cracking down on roving prisoner gangs, but when Andersonville was liberated by Brigadier General James H. Wilson's cavalry expedition in April 1865, Wirz was arrested. He was brought before a military tribunal in the Civil War's only war crimes trial, convicted, and executed. He was in reality

STATISTICS ON PRISONERS

	UNION	CONFEDERATE
Total Prisoners	215,000–220,000	200,000–211,000
Prisoner Deaths	22,600	26,500

PEAK POPULATIONS OF MAJOR PRISONS

	UNION	CONFEDERATE
Andersonville		32,000
Belle Isle		10,000
Camp Chase	10,000	
Elmira Prison	12,122	
Fort Delaware	8,000	
Point Lookout	20,000	
Rock Island	7,149	
Salisbury		10,000

RIGHT Libby Prison in Richmond was a former warehouse separated from other buildings, making it easy to guard. A tunnel dug by the prisoners led to a February 9, 1864 escape, but almost half of the 109 Federal officers involved were recaptured.

RIGHT Federal prisoners play baseball, a favorite pastime of Civil War soldiers, at the Salisbury, North Carolina, prison. The Confederate government purchased an abandoned cotton factory to house prisoners of the Provost Marshall. Later, Union prisoners were brought there and conditions were good for a time until overcrowding deteriorated them.

BELOW This photograph shows part of the stockade at Andersonville, with its tent city and a portion of the "dead line" shown in the foreground. Lack of food, sanitation, and shelter led to death or the emaciated condition found in survivors.

prisoners in camps grew dramatically. The Confederate prison at Salisbury, North Carolina, had a mortality rate of 25 percent. The largest Southern facilities in the early part of the war were Richmond's Libby Prison for officers, and Belle Isle for enlisted men and noncommissioned officers. At Belle Isle, in the middle of the James River, tents were the only shelter available to the captives.

Yet Northern prisons were not beyond reproach. The quasi-governmental soldiers' relief organization, the U.S. Sanitary Commission, cited poor conditions at Northern camps, even at the spacious Camp Douglas near Chicago. The prison at Elmira, New York had the highest mortality rate of Northern prisons, equal to Salisbury's 25 percent.

Point Lookout, Maryland, held large numbers of Confederate prisoners. Lieutenant General Jubal Early had hoped to liberate the prisoners there during his 1864 raid on Washington, but the plan was aborted before it was launched. Fort Delaware on the Delaware River near Wilmington had a stockade for enlisted men similar to that at Andersonville, while senior officers were held in an imposing masonry fort building. Fort Delaware's strict discipline and harsh conditions during the winter gave it the reputation of being the North's Andersonville.

a scapegoat for the inadequacies of the entire Southern prisoner-of-war system, which by the end of the war had difficulty providing for its own soldiers in the field, let alone for camp inmates.

Andersonville was not the only prison with intolerable conditions. After the system for exchanging prisoners which functioned early in the war broke down the number of

THE WAR CRIME TRIAL OF HENRY WIRZ

Heinrich Wirz's three-month trial saw inconsistent testimony and post-war hysteria weigh heavily in the outcome. His rough manner and disfigured right arm made Wirz resemble the monster he was portrayed as in the North. Just before his death sentence was to be carried out, Wirz was approached by a secret War Department agent who offered a reprieve in exchange for a statement implicating Jefferson Davis in prisoner murders at Andersonville. Wirz refused to cooperate in this lie and was executed.

THE EXPERIENCE OF THE U.S.C.T.

THE UNITED STATES Colored Troops or U.S.C.T. was the designation given to Federal regiments of African-American soldiers, led primarily by white officers. The U.S. Congress authorized the enlistment of African-Americans in July 1862, and some started to see action later that year.

More than 186,000 African-Americans enlisted in the Union army. On January 1, 1865, there were more African-Americans in the Federal army than there were Confederate soldiers. By the end of the war, U.S.C.T. troops had served in all theaters of the war—east, west, and south.

During the summer of 1863 an attempt was made by Federal Rear Admiral John Dahlgren and Brigadier General Quincy Gillmore to recapture or silence the guns of Fort Sumter in Charleston. The Federals occupied Folly Island, but had to take Morris Island on the extreme southeastern lip of Charleston Harbor to bring guns within range of Fort Sumter's vulnerable gorge wall. An infantry assault was launched on July 10, led by Brigadier General George C. Strong. The Federals overran Rebel rifle pits on Morris Island, but were faced with staggering fire from an earthen fortification known as Battery or Fort Wagner and turned back. The next day a similar assault was halted.

Despite the failures, Gillmore, on July 18, made one more attempt with a supporting bombardment from land and sea. General Strong chose a newly arrived regiment, the 54th Massachusetts, to be the vanguard of the attack. The 54th, a regiment of free African-Americans led by white officers, eagerly sought the chance to see action. Their commander was 25-year-old Colonel Robert Gould Shaw, who had raised and trained the regiment himself. At twilight, the 54th advanced, forced to march in tight formation along the narrow beach. Many reached the top of the parapet, where a hand-to-hand struggle occurred, but Shaw and most of the regiment was cut down. Other units followed the inspired lead of the 54th

ABOVE A recruitment poster encourages ex-slaves and free African-Americans to join in the defense of the Union.

Massachusetts, but Fort Wagner could not be taken. After weeks of siege operations against it, the fort was abandoned by the Rebels. The attack on July 18 resulted in 1,515 Federal casualties compared with just 174 for the Confederates.

In early 1864, Gillmore began an operation to take Florida, and cut the Confederate supply lines from the state. The mission foundered when Brigadier General Truman Seymour's force, which included the 54th Massachusetts and another African-American regiment, was spectacularly defeated by a Confederate force composed mostly of home guards at the Battle of Olustee on February 20.

In the attack on Petersburg, Virginia, on June 18, 1864, a part of Major General Ambrose Burnside's IX Corps seized ground some 500 feet from the Confederate line. Colonel Henry Pleasants, who commanded the 48th Pennsylvania, a regiment composed of men from the coal-mining region of that state, got permission to dig a mine or gallery under the

BELOW The band of the 107th U.S.C.T. at Fort Corcoran, Arlington, VA. The brass instruments held by the musicians—cornets and saxhorns—were the mainstays of the military brass band.

"The Old Flag Never Touched the Ground, Boys."

MEDAL OF HONOR WINNER WILLIAM H. CARNEY, WHO SAVED THE COLORS OF THE 54TH MASSACHUSETTS IN THE ATTACK ON FORT WAGNER

LEFT Sgt. Major Christian A. Fleetwood of the IV U.S.C.T. was color bearer of the regiment at the Battle of Chaffin's Farm, or New Market Heights, near Richmond in September 1864. He received the Medal of Honor for bravery during the battle.

Confederate position. The work began on June 25, and by July 23 it was completed.

Burnside had been drilling troops to spearhead the attack. They were in the African-American division of Brigadier General Edward Ferrero. The Army of the Potomac commander, Major General Meade, saw the potential, should the operation fail, for the press to exploit the sacrifice of African-American soldiers at a time when the Lincoln administration was already under heavy political fire. Lieutenant General U.S. Grant agreed. Burnside then had his other three division commanders draw lots to determine who would lead the attack, and Brigadier General James Ledlie, the weakest, won.

At 4.40 a.m. on July 30, the mine exploded and more than 240 Confederate soldiers were killed outright. Giant clods of earth rained down among the Union troops, but 15 minutes passed before they advanced. Untrained Federal troops, without the leadership of Ledlie, who remained in a bombproof shelter, came forward. They stopped to gawk at the destruction as the Confederates began to rally. Burnside's other two white divisions followed, all crowding into the crater.

Finally, Ferrero's division was ordered forward, but the African-American soldiers, who were trained for the operation, were blocked in their advance by the inexperienced white troops. They began to push forward but Rebel Brigadier General William Mahone mounted a successful counterattack. By 9.00 a.m., Meade was convinced that the attack was a failure and ordered Burnside to suspend it. As a result of the disaster at the Battle of the Crater, Burnside was relieved of command.

At the end of September 1864, the Army of the James stormed Rebel Fort Harrison and captured New Market Heights. U.S.C.T. soldiers won 14 Medals of Honor for bravery in the action. The Confederates fended off attacks on Fort Gilmer, but the action at New Market Heights forced Lee to extend and reinforce his lines around Richmond, taxing his already limited resources.

U.S.C.T. soldiers played major roles in defeating General John Bell Hood's Tennessee offensive at the Battle of Nashville on December 15 and 16, 1864. They also fought effectively in operations against Fort Blakeley on April 9, 1865, as Federals completed the investment of Mobile, Alabama.

WILLIAM H. CARNEY

As a member of the 54th Massachusetts Regiment, Sergeant William H. Carney served as color bearer. The July 18, 1863 attack on Charleston Harbor's Fort Morris by the 54th resulted in 281 casualties for the regiment. Carney was the first African-American to receive the Medal of Honor from the U.S. Army for recovering the Federal colors in the hand-to-hand struggle. After the battle he proudly described the action, "The old flag never touched the ground, boys."

RIGHT These determined African-American soldiers, seen here in a shot staged for the camera, were pickets at Dutch Gap Canal, a failed project started by Maj. Gen. Benjamin Butler to bypass Rebel guns at Drewry's Bluff, near Richmond.

SIEGE OF RICHMOND AND PETERSBURG

STALEMATE OF SIEGE warfare, brought about by the stubborn Rebel resistance at Richmond and Petersburg, had consistently saved the capital from capture. The Federals in Virginia were not content just to wait out the end as Union victories elsewhere squeezed the life out of the Confederacy. Grant sought a way to break the siege at Petersburg, but his attention was drawn to the Shenandoah Valley.

Lieutenant General Jubal Early retained control of the valley after scattering the Federal forces opposing him. After a thrust toward the outskirts of Washington D.C. in July 1864, Early returned to the valley, forcing Grant to send Philip H. Sheridan to reorganize Federal forces and go after the Rebel commander, whom he hammered at Winchester on September 19, and again at Fisher's Hill on the 22nd. Early retreated to Staunton, and Sheridan abandoned the pursuit, instead focusing on the destruction of crops that supplied the Rebel forces around Richmond.

Early cautiously followed Sheridan north. On October 19, while Sheridan was returning from Washington, Early hit the Federal camps. The Northerners were driven back; but their commanders held steady and Sheridan returned to the camp as the battle began, allowing the Union forces to reorganize and launch a furious counterattack. The Rebels retired from the field and never again mounted an offensive in the Shenandoah Valley. Victory at Cedar Creek helped cement Lincoln's reelection and cut supply lines to the Confederate army holding Petersburg and Richmond.

On the Petersburg front, the Federals launched an offensive southeast of Richmond at New Market Heights and Fort Harrison on September 30 but failed to take Fort Gilmer. At the same time, the Army of the Potomac extended its line outside Petersburg west toward the Southside Railroad, but was checked at Peeble's Farm. A further push west was attempted in late

June 1864 – April 1865

THE QUARTERMASTER CORPS

A major reason for Northern victory was the ability of the quartermaster corps, led by Montgomery Meigs, to keep Union military forces supplied. Millions of tons of food, ammunition, weapons, and other goods were purchased and distributed to forces in the field. The Confederates, due to limited financing, manufacturing, and transportation options, could not keep pace in supplying its forces, though ordnance chief Josiah Gorgas and European agents James Bulloch and Caleb Huse made valiant efforts to do so.

October, but Major General Winfield S. Hancock's II Corps was defeated at Burgess's Mill.

The winter was extremely difficult on Lee's soldiers, who endured life in the trenches with little food and inadequate shelter. The Federals, on the other hand, were supplied by a specially built railroad from the Union depot at City Point. In early February, Grant made another attempt to turn the Rebel right flank by moving forward to the Boydton Plank Road. On the afternoon of February 5, a Rebel counterattack at the Battle of Hatcher's Run stopped his advance. However, Grant was still able to extend his siege line two miles farther west.

Lee learned of the defeat of Johnston's remaining Confederate forces south of Virginia at Bentonville, North Carolina, on March 19–21 and understood this meant that Sherman would continue north to Virginia, cutting off any attempt to unite Lee's army with Johnston's. Lee decided to abandon Petersburg before Sherman could prevent his escape south.

BELOW Ruins of the Gallego Flour Mills along the James River in Richmond. Federal forces never got close enough to the city to cause significant damage. These buildings burned as part of a general conflagration started by retreating Rebels and looters as the city was abandoned on the night of April 2–3, 1865.

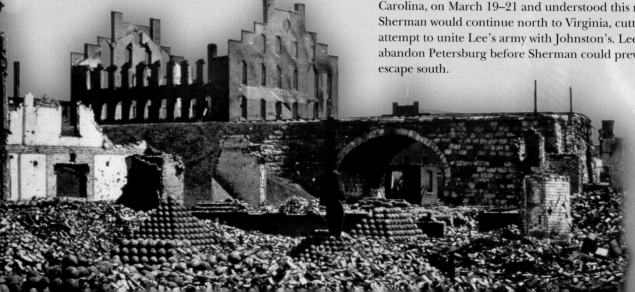

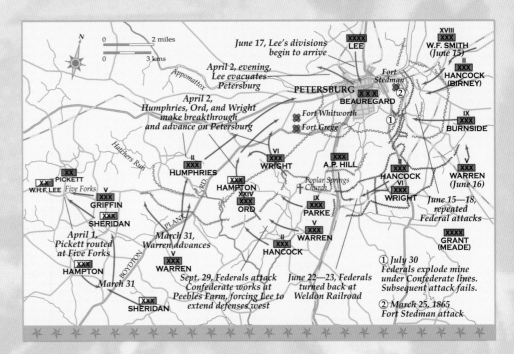

RIGHT Major actions in the nearly ten-month struggle at Petersburg. After Federal assaults on June 15–16, 1864 failed to dislodge the Confederates from their prepared defense line at Petersburg, soldiers from Gen. Robert E. Lee's Army of Northern Virginia arrived to occupy the trenches. The Federals countered with a line east and south of the Rebels and Lt. Gen. U.S. Grant ordered advances to extend the line to the west. Finally, after a failed breakout attempt at Fort Stedman on March 25, 1865, and defeat of a large part of his army at Five Forks on April 1, 1865, Lee evacuated Petersburg.

BACKGROUND President Lincoln tours Richmond on April 3, 1865 shortly after Federal forces entered the city, restored order, and got control of the fires that burned part of the city during the night.

To lead the attack Lee selected Major General John B. Gordon, a proven fighter. On March 25, Gordon launched a surprise attack and succeeded in taking Fort Stedman and nearby Federal batteries. But at Fort Haskell, Union forces rallied, stalling the Rebel attack until reinforcements arrived. Lee finally called off the attack, but the Federals were able to advance part of their line. Fort Stedman was a disastrous setback for Lee's plans to gain an advantage on Grant and effect an orderly evacuation of Petersburg and Richmond.

Grant now attempted to extend his forces to the west to cut the Boydton Plank Road and the Southside Railroad. The Federal cavalry, led by Philip Sheridan, advanced to Dinwiddie Court House, threatening to turn the right flank of the Confederate line, and Lee sent a force to counter him. On the 31st, a Confederate force of infantry and cavalry under Major General George Pickett attacked Sheridan's cavalry, driving them back, and then establishing a defensive line along White Oak Road at Five Forks. Confident the Federals would not attack on April 1, Pickett and his senior officers left the immediate area for a meal. At 4.00 p.m. the Federal V Corps and Sheridan's dismounted cavalry descended on the Rebel line at Five Forks, shattering it in under an hour.

The Battle of Five Forks was considered the "Waterloo of the Confederacy." Learning of Sheridan's success, Grant launched an all-out attack on the Petersburg defenders early on April 2. Lee knew the time had come to evacuate Petersburg and Richmond. He informed Davis by telegram, and panic quickly spread as government officials and frightened citizens boarded trains for Danville, Virginia.

Order was restored by Federal troops who entered Richmond on the morning of April 3, with units of the African-American XXV Corps in the vanguard. The Army of the Potomac marched into Petersburg on the heels of the retreating Army of Northern Virginia. President Lincoln, who had been spending several weeks with Grant at City Point, toured Richmond on the 3rd with Rear Admiral David D. Porter. Lincoln admired a statue of George Washington and cracked a joke about the hasty flight of the Confederate President to the southwest, "Washington is looking at me and pointing at Jeff Davis."

LEFT One of the hundreds of casualties in the long campaign at Petersburg was this Confederate soldier.

ABOVE LEFT President Abraham Lincoln reads his second inaugural address in front of the U.S. Capitol on March 4, 1865. In the audience was John Wilkes Booth.

SURRENDER AT APPOMATTOX

WILMER MCLEAN had brought his family to the gentle rolling pastures of Appomattox County, Virginia, in 1863. McLean sought the peace and quiet of farming in one of the few areas of Virginia not torn apart by years of devastating war. In April 1865, Union and Rebel soldiers would literally end up at McLean's doorstep.

After the fall of Petersburg, which followed the "Waterloo of the Confederacy" at Five Forks, General Robert E. Lee hoped to withdraw his forces to the west on April 3, in order to begin a march south to rendezvous with the force commanded by General Joseph E. Johnston. But his army needed food, and although supplies were reported to be on rail cars at Amelia Court House, those cars contained only ammunition. Lee then sent his men into the countryside to forage for food. But they were running out of time. Grant ordered Major General Philip Sheridan's cavalry to pursue the remnants of Lee's army, blocking their intended route and forcing Lee to change his army's heading due west to Lynchburg.

On April 5, Lee found Sheridan's cavalry blocking the road to Lynchburg. The Rebels turned north and the next day, April 6, the Federals attacked Lee's rear-guard, which was accompanying the wagon trains along a stream called Sayler's Creek. Although fighting broke out in several sectors, the Federals prevailed, and at Sayler's Creek Lee lost one-quarter of his remaining force in the last major action of the Army of Northern Virginia.

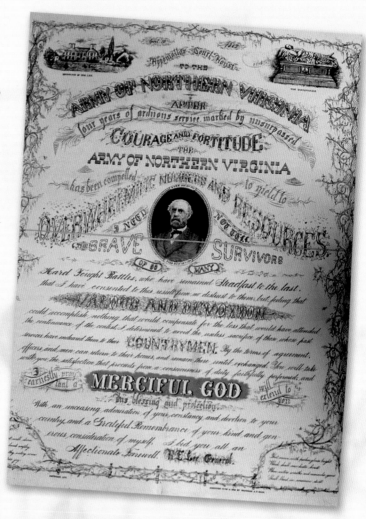

April 9, 1865

ABOVE A commemorative copy of Lee's Farewell Address, a stirring and brilliant adieu to his troops. After the Civil War Lee urged Southerners to put bitterness aside and move forward. Though deprived of his citizenship in the post-war period of frantic reconstruction, Lee would soon join the ranks of lasting American heroes.

THE LAST BATTLES

As the Army of Northern Virginia was fighting its last battles, action in other theaters also wound down. Sherman's army group advanced north through the Carolinas and defeated forces assembled by General Johnston at Bentonville, North Carolina, March 19–21. The final resistance at Mobile was broken with Federal victories at Spanish Fort and Fort Blakeley in early April. Scattered fighting continued in the Trans-Mississippi region, with the last battle of the war occurring at Palmito Ranch, Texas, May 12–13, 1865.

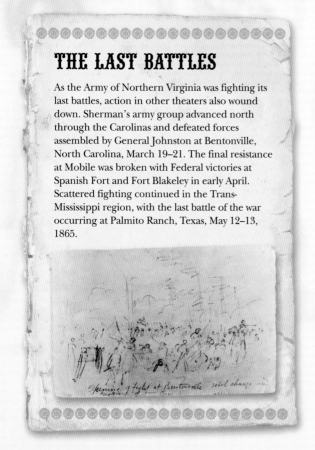

The following day, Grant sent a message to Lee under a flag of truce, proposing surrender terms to the Rebels struggling toward Lynchburg. A dialog started, but Grant was unwilling to accept Lee's proposal for a restoration of peace, and the negotiations broke down. On Palm Sunday morning, April 9, Lee's exhausted soldiers attempted to break through Sheridan's troopers, blocking the road at Appomattox Court House. Two corps of infantry backed up Sheridan, virtually surrounding the Confederates. Lee rejected the idea that his army take to the hills to fight a guerrilla war. He initiated an exchange of messages with Grant asking for surrender terms.

ABOVE The home of Wilmer McLean, Appomattox Court House, Virginia. The end of four long years of war effectively came in the parlor of this house, with the surrender of the Army of Northern Virginia.

That same afternoon, Lee and Grant met in the parlor of Wilmer McLean's house, just across the square from Appomattox Court House. Grant later recalled his thoughts: "What General Lee's feelings were, I do not know, as he was a man with much dignity with an impassable face, it was impossible to say whether he felt inwardly glad that the end had finally come, or felt sad over the result and was too manly to feel it. But my own feelings, which had been quite jubilant on the receipt of the letter, were sad and depressed. I felt like anything rather than rejoicing at the downfall of the foe which fought so long and valiantly and suffered so much for the cause. The cause was, I believe, one of the worst for which a people ever fought I do not question, however, the sincerity of the great mass of those who were opposed to us."

On April 12, the Federal army marched into the square at Appomattox Court House. Soon, the tattered but proud Rebel soldiers filed between solemn lines of Union soldiers, stacked their arms and furled their flags. The war in Virginia was over. The end of the Confederacy was not far behind.

OTHER SURRENDERS

After Appomattox, other Confederate forces began to lay down arms. Johnston surrendered the second largest Rebel army to Sherman in North Carolina on April 26. News of this and Jefferson Davis's flight forced Richard Taylor's surrender in Alabama on May 4. While some Confederates in the Trans-Mississippi (seen below) fled to Mexico hoping to revive the struggle, Simon Buckner ended official resistance there on May 26 in New Orleans. The last Confederate general to surrender was Cherokee leader Stand Watie, on June 23, 1865.

RIGHT This modern painting corrects errors in previous portrayals of the scene inside the McLean parlor on April 8, 1865. Lt. Gen. Ulysses S. Grant shakes hands with Gen. Robert E. Lee as officers of the Army of the Potomac look on and aids attend to the letters detailing terms.

BACKGROUND Confederate stragglers signal their willingness to give up as Federal cavalry puruses Lee's columns at Amelia Court House on April 5.

LINCOLN'S ASSASSINATION

AFTER SPENDING two weeks at the Petersburg front, Abraham Lincoln returned to Washington on April 9. Late that day, he received news of General Robert E. Lee's surrender at Appomattox. Crowds clamored for his appearance, and Lincoln promised to deliver a major speech on Tuesday, April 11, which he did that evening from the portico of the White House, then known as the Executive Mansion. With the war coming to a close, Lincoln spoke about the problems that would confront the nation, as the states of the Confederacy were reincorporated into the Union.

A major part of his speech was devoted to the reconstruction of the South, a controversial political issue in Washington, and on how the freed slaves would fit into that new order. Lincoln hinted that those freed slaves would share political power with whites in the South. This idea was at the time an emotive and challenging issue for Northerners and Southerners alike. In the audience was John Wilkes Booth, a handsome Maryland-born actor popular in Washington circles, who had great sympathy for the Southern cause. When Booth heard Lincoln's reconstruction plans in the speech, he turned to his friend Lewis Powell and was later quoted as saying, "… that is the last speech he will ever make."

April 14 and 15, 1865

ABOVE In this period lithograph, John Wilkes Booth jumps from the President's box at Ford's Theatre to the stage below, a distance of 12 feet.

BELOW LEFT The assassination of Abraham Lincoln rocked the nation in 1865 and details of the tragedy were recorded in newspapers throughout the North.

Booth was staying at a small Washington boarding house on H Street operated by Mary Surratt, after being introduced to her son, John, a Confederate agent. For months Booth had been in contact with the Confederate secret service and had discussed a plan to kidnap Lincoln and hold him to ransom. Present at various meetings were school friends Samuel Arnold and Michael O'Laughlin, pharmacist David Herold, the Rebel deserter and agent Powell, also known as Lewis T. Paine, who was physically powerful but mentally disabled, and George Atzerodt. The President's movements were published in the newspaper, but Lincoln often changed his plans, scuttling Booth's kidnap attempts.

On the evening of Good Friday, April 14, Abraham Lincoln, his wife, and two guests, Major Henry Rathbone and his fiancée, Miss Clara Harris, attended Ford's Theatre on 10th Street to see Laura Keene in *Our American Cousin*, a comedy. Booth, a regular at John Ford's playhouse, had learned of this earlier in the day. Paine, Atzerodt, and Booth planned simultaneous attempts on the lives of Secretary of State Seward, Vice-President Andrew Johnston, and Lincoln.

FAR LEFT One lead ball from this .44-caliber derringer was enough to mortally wound the President. Booth was an experienced and confident marksman and the range was favorable for the single-shot weapon.

RIGHT The bodies of the four co-conspirators who were sentenced to death for their involvement in Lincoln's assassination dangle from the temporary gallows constructed at Washington's Old Penitentiary shortly after the execution was carried out on the afternoon of July 7, 1865. From left to right are Mrs. Surratt, Paine, Herold, and Atzerodt in this photograph by famed Civil War photographer Alexander Gardner.

BELOW
John T. Ford's Theatre on 10th Street in Washington, D.C. opened in August 1863 and was a popular venue. While checking his mail on the 14th, Booth learned that the Lincolns would attend the performance there that night rather than a special performance at Grover's Theatre, as Booth and most of Washington expected.

BACKGROUND Thousands of mourners witness the funeral procession of President Abraham Lincoln down Pennsylvania Avenue in Washington on April 19, 1865.

Lincoln had toiled hard for four years to solve America's greatest crisis. His wisdom, patience, and patriotism were gifts to the country. His dedication to freedom was the impetus for a people to overcome grave internal problems and go on to create the greatest nation the world has ever known.

At about 10.15 p.m. Booth approached the door to the Presidential box. Because Ulysses S. Grant had declined an invitation to the play—the shy Grant wanted to avoid public attention and Julia Grant had been derided by Mary Todd Lincoln during the President's visit to Petersburg—there was no military escort at Ford's Theatre, only Lincoln's bodyguard, who, perhaps with the President's knowledge, had stepped away. Booth opened the door, shot Lincoln once in the back of the head, slashed the unarmed Rathbone with a hunting knife, and leaped 12 feet to the stage below. Booth's spur caught in a U.S. Treasury Guard's flag on the way down and he severely injured his leg. He limped out of the rear exit and escaped on a horse held for him by stagehand Edman Spangler.

The unconscious Lincoln was brought across the street to the house of William Petersen, a tailor, where military doctors attended him. Members of the government arrived throughout the night. The other two assassination attempts failed—Atzerodt lost his nerve; and Paine was overpowered before reaching the bedridden Seward. Abraham Lincoln died at 7.22 a.m. on April 15.

After Lincoln's death, there was a spasm of grief and anger throughout the North. Booth was killed on April 26 in a Virginia tobacco barn by a posse of Federal soldiers. His co-conspirators and associates were tried by a military tribunal, convicted, and imprisoned or executed. After a momentous funeral procession through Washington and other cities, in which more than seven million Americans turned out to see the Presidential coffin and funeral train, Abraham Lincoln was laid to rest on May 4, in Springfield, Illinois.

COST OF THE WAR

CASUALTIES

620,000 soldiers, sailors, and marines killed from all causes; 1,094,453 total military casualties

Approximately 50,000 civilian war-related deaths in the South

One Presidential assassination

FINANCIAL

Cost of the War to the U.S. Government—$6.19 billion

Cost of the War to the Confederate Government—$2.1 billion

Total Economic Cost to the Seceding States—Incalculable